Alexander Graham Bell

These and other titles are included in The Importance Of biography series:

Alexander the Great	Adolf Hitler
Muhammad Ali	Harry Houdini
Maya Angelou	Thomas Jefferson
Louis Armstrong	Mother Jones
James Baldwin	Chief Joseph
Clara Barton	John F. Kennedy
The Beatles	Martin Luther King Jr.
Alexander Graham Bell	Joe Louis
Napoleon Bonaparte	Douglas MacArthur
Julius Caesar	Malcolm X
Rachel Carson	Thurgood Marshall
Charlie Chaplin	Margaret Mead
Charlemagne	Golda Meir
Cesar Chavez	Michelangelo
Winston Churchill	Wolfgang Amadeus
Cleopatra	Mozart
Christopher Columbus	John Muir
Hernando Cortes	Sir Isaac Newton
Marie Curie	Richard M. Nixon
Leonardo Da Vinci	Georgia O'Keeffe
Charles Dickens	Louis Pasteur
Emily Dickinson	Pablo Picasso
Walt Disney	Elvis Presley
Amelia Earhart	Jackie Robinson
Thomas Edison	Norman Rockwell
Albert Einstein	Eleanor Roosevelt
Duke Ellington	Anwar Sadat
F. Scott Fitzgerald	Margaret Sanger
Dian Fossey	Oskar Schindler
Anne Frank	William Shakespeare
Benjamin Franklin	John Steinbeck
Galileo Galilei	Tecumseh
Emma Goldman	Mother Teresa
Jane Goodall	Jim Thorpe
Martha Graham	Mark Twain
Lorraine Hansberry	Queen Victoria
Stephen Hawking	Pancho Villa
Ernest Hemingway	Simon Wiesenthal
Jim Henson	H. G. Wells

Alexander Graham Bell

by Robyn M. Weaver

Lucent Books, P.O. Box 289011, San Diego, CA 92198-9011

For Andrew and Samantha . . .
who possess the wisdom to wonder,
and relish in the magic it brings.

Library of Congress Cataloging-in-Publication Data

Weaver, Robyn M.
    The importance of Alexander Graham Bell / by Robyn M. Weaver.
        p.   cm. — (The importance of series)
    Includes bibliographical references and index.
    Summary: Examines the life and work of the man known as
the inventor of the telephone, discussing his family, education, his
various inventions, and his work with the deaf.
    ISBN 1-56006-603-2 (lib. bdg. : alk. paper)
    1. Bell, Alexander Graham, 1847–1922 Juvenile literature.
2. Inventors—United States Biography Juvenile literature.
[1. Bell, Alexander Graham, 1847–1922. 2. Inventors.] I. Title.
II. Series: Importance of.
TK6143.B4W43 2000
621.385' 092—dc21
[B]

                                                    99-29706
                                                       CIP

Copyright 2000 by Lucent Books, Inc., P.O. Box 289011,
San Diego, California 92198-9011

Printed in the U.S.A.

Contents

Foreword

THE IMPORTANCE OF biography series deals with individuals who have made a unique contribution to history. The editors of the series have deliberately chosen to cast a wide net and include people from all fields of endeavor. Individuals from politics, music, art, literature, philosophy, science, sports, and religion are all represented. In addition, the editors did not restrict the series to individuals whose accomplishments have helped change the course of history. Of necessity, this criterion would have eliminated many whose contribution was great, though limited. Charles Darwin, for example, was responsible for radically altering the scientific view of the natural history of the world. His achievements continue to impact the study of science today. Others, such as Chief Joseph of the Nez Percé, played a pivotal role in the history of their own people. While Joseph's influence does not extend much beyond the Nez Percé, his nonviolent resistance to white expansion and his continuing role in protecting his tribe and his homeland remain an inspiration to all.

These biographies are more than factual chronicles. Each volume attempts to emphasize an individual's contributions both in his or her own time and for posterity. For example, the voyages of Christopher Columbus opened the way to European colonization of the New World. Unquestionably, his encounter with the New World brought monumental changes to both Europe and the Americas in his day. Today, however, the broader impact of Columbus's voyages is being critically scrutinized. *Christopher Columbus,* as well as every biography in The Importance Of series, includes and evaluates the most recent scholarship available on each subject.

Each author includes a wide variety of primary and secondary source quotations to document and substantiate his or her work. All quotes are footnoted to show readers exactly how and where biographers derive their information, as well as provide stepping stones to further research. These quotations enliven the text by giving readers eyewitness views of the life and times of each individual covered in The Importance Of series.

Finally, each volume is enhanced by photographs, bibliographies, chronologies, and comprehensive indexes. For both the casual reader and the student engaged in research, The Importance Of biographies will be a fascinating adventure into the lives of people who have helped shape humanity's past and present, and who will continue to shape its future.

IMPORTANT DATES IN THE LIFE OF ALEXANDER GRAHAM BELL

1847
Bell is born on March 3 in Edinburgh, Scotland.

1872
Opens his own School of Vocal Physiology in Boston and begins working on a multiple telegraph.

1877
Marries Mabel Hubbard; forms the Bell Telephone Company with early backers.

1871
Moves to Boston; teaches at the Boston School for the Deaf.

1862
Travels to London to live with his grandfather.

1875
Forms formal partnership with Gardiner Greene Hubbard and Thomas Sanders.

|1845|1850|1860|1870|1875|

1863
Teaches his first class at Weston House Academy in Elgin, Scotland.

1874
Conceives idea for telephone and meets Thomas Watson.

1858
Chooses Graham as middle name.

1868
Teaches speech to the deaf at Susanna E. Hull's school for deaf children in London.

1876
Utters famous, "Watson, come here"; receives patent for the telephone.

1879
Settles with Western Union for rights to telephone.

1901
Invents the tetrahedral kite.

1907
Forms the Aerial Experiment Association (AEA) with three other men.

1898
Is elected as a regent of the Smithsonian Institution.

1883
Sponsors *Science* with Hubbard; is elected to the National Academy of Sciences.

1922
Dies and is laid to rest in Beinn Bhreagh, Nova Scotia.

1880	1890	1900	1910	1920

1915
First transcontinental telephone call.

1887
Meets six-year-old Helen Keller.

1908
Takes photograph of the AEA's *Silver Dart*, the first heavier-than-air machine in Canada.

1880
Wins French Volta Prize for scientific achievement.

1919
Hydrofoil craft he helped invent sets a world marine speed record.

1890
Forms the American Association to Promote Teaching of Speech to the Deaf.

1897
Accepts the position of president of the National Geographic Society.

Communication and Invention

Calling a parent after soccer practice, logging onto the Internet, and sending a fax are all possible because of the accomplishments of Alexander Graham Bell. His original machine that reproduced speech—which he first called a talking telegraph—is what we now call the telephone. It used electricity to reproduce human speech and has become the basis for today's many forms of mass communication.

Bell's invention has evolved into a tool that allows businesses and financial institutions to transfer money electronically in their day-to-day operations. It allows family members who are separated by great distances to stay in touch through long distance telephone calls or e-mail communication. It allows doctors to fax medical records, which helps them provide better health care during emergencies.

As the editors of *Time for Biography* state, nearly the entire world is dependent on the telephone today:

Few Americans—indeed, few members of most of the world's nations—can imagine life without the telephone. It is considered a daily essential like food, housing, clothing. But people haven't always had telephones, and the struggle of Alexander Graham Bell (1847–1922) is a tale of heartbreaking work and courageous dedication. The devotion of his wife and the loyalty of

Because of Alexander Graham Bell's scientific genius, people today can communicate with each other from almost anywhere.

Though Bell faced many personal hardships, family support and hard work contributed to his ultimate success.

his friend and fellow inventor, Thomas Watson, kept Bell from total despair.[1]

Although many inventors tried to reproduce speech over wires, Alexander Graham Bell was the first to successfully build a working telephone. The telephone of today does not look anything like Bell's first invention; however, it is a tangible reminder of the worldwide communication available because of Bell's original crude device. This fact was first reflected by Professor F. A. P. Barnard of Columbia University when he said: "The name of the inventor of the telephone would be handed down to posterity with a permanent claim on the gratitude and remembrance of mankind."[2]

Bell's contributions to communication did not begin or end with the telephone, though. He was a student and teacher of speech, as were his father and grandfather. He devoted many more years to his career as a teacher than he did to the time he spent inventing the telephone.

A curiosity about sound and speech was only one of the many infatuations Bell had during his varied life of research and inventions. Later, he became a founder of the National Geographic Society as well as a contributor to its magazine. His interest in the organization stemmed from his desire to continue to research new inventions and fund other inventors who had inquisitive minds like his.

Bell and other inventors interested in the mechanics of flight began one of the first aviation groups in North America. This fascination with flight prompted Bell to help finance the group's many experiments with kites and other flying apparatuses. They accomplished many exciting firsts in aviation history.

Even as age caused him to cut back on his own inventions, Bell continued to encourage and fund his fellow inventors. He never forgot the struggles involved with building, adjusting, and experimenting on that first

The telephone has revolutionized modern society by allowing people to communicate over long distances instantaneously.

telephone. Many times during that process of creating, he often lacked the funds to purchase necessary materials for the project. Some biographers believe that Bell's support of other inventors was as important to modern technology as his first telephone.

In the past century, Alexander Graham Bell has been recognized as the premiere inventor of the telephone. Those who knew him well, however, remember Bell for his love of thinking and wondering as well as for his researching and teaching capabilities. Even after inventing the telephone, when Bell was asked to put his oc-cupation on official forms and documents, he would write, "teacher of the deaf."[3] One of his most famous pupils, Helen Keller, gave Bell credit for her successful career as a writer and a speaker.

But it is the telephone that Bell invented that he is remembered for most often. Historians agree that Bell's telephone has had an overwhelming influence on modern society, and it continues to impact daily life. This influence would not be possible without the first telephone, and for that accomplishment, Alexander Graham Bell remains a giant in the field of communication.

1 A Family of Communicators

Alexander Graham Bell was surrounded by people who were devoted to the study of sound and speech. His father and grandfather lectured audiences and individuals regarding proper speech. As a hobby, the two men also enjoyed giving dramatic readings of popular authors'

Alexander Graham Bell grew up in a family fascinated with sound and speech.

works. With two generations already immersed in the study of sound and speech, it was only natural for the next Alexander Bell to also take an interest in the family trade and pursue the study of sound as a career.

His Parents and Their Influence

On a chilly spring day in Edinburgh, Scotland, Alexander Bell was born on March 3, 1847. Aleck, as his family called him, was the second son of Alexander Melville Bell and his wife, Eliza Symonds Bell.

Alexander Melville Bell was an elocutionist, a person who taught the proper enunciation of words and the necessities of public speaking. As a teacher, Aleck's father had so many successful students that his name soon became recognized around the world as an expert at identifying and solving speech problems.

Later, his father's research and writing efforts about elocution won him further praise as an author. By 1892 his book *The Standard Elocutionist* had gone into its 168th printing in England alone. Nearly 1 million copies had been sold around the world by the time the book finally went out of print.

Part of Alexander Melville Bell's success came from his outgoing nature. His exuberant personality encouraged an atmosphere full of energy and an attitude full of spirit. His students and colleagues enjoyed his dramatic flair when he taught or gave readings. One biographer says that his exuberant character was emphasized by his outrageous clothes: "Melville, known for his theatrical flair . . . often sported plaid pants or curious hats, and even an occasional kilt."[4]

Aleck's mother, however, leaned toward a quieter manner regarding her interests. Eliza, who was ten years older than her husband, was known in Edinburgh as a superb painter of miniatures. The couple met in 1843, after Melville had commissioned a portrait of himself. They married the same year, and Eliza continued to paint throughout her long life.

As one biographer notes, it was soon apparent that her disposition and views of life differed from Melville's:

> In outlook, she was much different from Aleck's father—deeply religious and observant where he was careless of the strict Scottish Sabbath rules and somewhat skeptical—but their marriage seems to have been blissfully calm.[5]

In spite of their obvious differences, the marriage was strong. Both parents encouraged young Aleck's schooling, al-

Bell's father emanated vitality and energy. The exuberance he displayed in his work instilled a fascination with speech in his son.

though, true to their personalities, they approached this task in different manners. Whereas his father was often harsh with criticism when he believed Aleck was not applying himself, his mother encouraged the boy's questioning mind.

It did not worry Eliza Bell to let Aleck roam the countryside, and she encouraged him to put on plays with his two brothers. All three of the boys enjoyed making up stories and acting them out, just as their father did in public. Although the family was not wealthy, they did maintain a comfortable standard of living and the boys had every educational advantage that their father's income and reputation could offer.

EARLY EDUCATION

Aleck, along with his older brother, Melly, and his younger brother, Edward, explored the Scottish countryside with enthusiasm, always anxious to see something new. Aleck loved to collect small items, such as plants, bones, and fossils, on his outdoor adventures, and he often brought them home. Although he was curious about his discoveries, he rarely bothered to research the items to learn their scientific names or to label them, as was a common academic

THE THREE ALEXANDER BELLS

Alexander Graham Bell was the third male in his family to be named Alexander Bell. Besides sharing a name with his father and grandfather, Bell also shared their love of teaching others about speech, as Thomas B. Costain explains in his book The Chord of Steel.

"It began with Alexander Bell, the grandfather, who was a shoemaker at St. Andrews, Scotland, in the early years of the nineteenth century. . . . He wanted to be an actor. He had a fine presence for the stage, although he was not tall. . . . Unfortunately the stage was regarded not only as 'low' in Scotland, but downright wicked. . . . He did the next best thing. He moved to Edinburgh and set himself up as a teacher in speech and elocution. . . .

The thwarted actor in Alexander the First came out in all his children, particularly in his second son . . . Alexander Melville. When in his early youth he was sent to Newfoundland for his health, he took advantage of a chance, first to organize a Shakespeare class and then to start the members on amateur theatricals. . . . The second Alexander Bell inherited the family traits and talents in superabundance. He was destined to reduce the teaching of proper speech to a science and to write a book called *Bell's Standard Elocutionist*, which came out in 1860. . . .

Alexander the Third, or perhaps it would be more to the point to call him Alexander the Great, was a Bell in many respects but in the most important aspect he went far beyond the other. To the rest of the family the teaching of proper speech was an end in itself. To the third of the line it was no more than a means to an end."

practice at the time. From his earliest years, Aleck had a passion for wondering about all the things he could see, touch, smell, and especially, hear.

Alexander Graham Bell's great-grandson, Edwin S. Grosvenor, tells a story about one of young Aleck's romps through the wheat fields south of Edinburgh. When the boy was only three or four, the family decided to have a picnic at Ferny Hill on the outskirts of town. Aleck ran off to play in the tall golden wheat covering the picnic area. His curly brown hair disappeared into the stalky grains that stood taller than his head. Hiding there, Aleck wondered if he could hear the wheat grow. Grosvenor writes,

> For a long time he sat listening intently to the silence. Then, in a panic, he realized he was lost in the dense wheat; he sobbed until he finally cried himself to sleep. "I was awakened by my father's voice," the boy would recall decades later. . . . Racing toward the sound, the wayward youngster was soon in his mother's arms. This was Alexander Graham Bell's first memory; for the remaining three score and ten years of his life, he would follow similar wanderings, driven by an impulsive nature and a deep curiosity of sound and silence.[6]

Even as a young boy, Aleck's mind was full of questions about sound and hearing. His mother, however, did not allow any of her sons to become consumed with only one area of education. As was the custom during that time, she taught her

A watercolor by Bell's mother shows Alexander (right), with his brothers Melville (left) and Edward.

boys the academic basics at home when they were young.

Eliza Bell even encouraged the boys to study during summer vacations at Milton Cottage, the family's country retreat at Trinity, Scotland. In this relaxed setting, the brothers read, explored, and even played tricks on each other. One of their favorite pranks included hiding and then sneaking up on an unsuspecting brother.

When Aleck was ten, he was enrolled in Royal High School, where he did not earn high grades in any classes. He did not take any science courses, and he hated Latin and Greek. On his days off from school, he relished in his own interests. He fashioned a personal museum for his collection of small animal bones and began reading about the stars.

Because of his father's flamboyant personality, Aleck's childhood was filled with many visitors, from world-renowned thinkers to nearby family members. On one such occasion, a student of Melville Bell's came to the household for a visit.

This young man was a Canadian named Alexander Graham. Young Aleck thought the man's name had a nice ring to it. He decided he did not like being referred to as the third Alexander Bell, and he chose a middle name for himself. On his eleventh birthday, he proclaimed that he would now be known as A. Graham Bell. His father honored his son's decision and raised his glass in a toast. From that day forward, every time that Aleck signed his name, it would read A. Graham Bell.

A GROWING INTEREST IN SOUND

Eliza Bell was hearing impaired and grew progressively worse as her sons matured. Most family photographs show Eliza holding an ear tube that she used to amplify sounds. An ear tube was a long hornlike instrument with a wide bell on one end that narrowed into a small earpiece at the other end. It was the most common aid for deaf people during this period of history.

Aleck's sensitivity toward his mother's deafness was often shown in the manner in which he communicated with her. Instead of raising his voice so she could hear from her ear tube, Aleck would press his lips against her forehead. He would gently speak so she could feel the formation of the words on her skin and interpret what he said.

In spite of her deteriorating hearing, Eliza played the piano remarkably well. She managed this talent by placing the small end of the ear tube into her mouth and the larger end on the top of the piano to feel the vibrations. Her love for music made an impression on young Aleck, and he learned to play the piano, too.

Before long it was apparent that Aleck had a true gift for the instrument, and his mother hired the much-sought-after pianist Auguste Benoit Bertini as his instructor. The well-known pianist personally tutored Aleck and, for a time, Aleck thought he might follow a career in music. Recalling that time of his life, Bell said, "My dream as a young man was to become a musician, and I used to smile in a superior way at the plans of my family to make something else of me."[7]

Melville Bell looks on as Elsie speaks to his wife through a speaking tube.

Despite his love for the piano, Aleck lost interest in playing the instrument when Bertini died, and he followed other dreams that would take him down different roads. Still, he enjoyed playing the piano throughout his life. His keen ear and talent proved beneficial as a teacher and helped him develop new ways to aid deaf children in feeling sound vibrations. Music also played a key role in the invention of the telephone; he used steel reeds in the early designs to reproduce musical tones.

FIRST EXPERIMENTS

Even though Aleck was passionate about sound and speech, his first experiment had nothing to do with either. The experiment did, however, help Aleck learn the process of trial and error, which would be instrumental to his success with the telephone.

One of Aleck's closest friends was Ben Herdman. Ben's father owned a flour mill where the two boys played daily and often found themselves in trouble for disrupting the workers. After one especially rough day of tolerating the boys' behavior, Ben's father encouraged them to do something useful. When they asked what he had in mind, Mr. Herdman shoved a bag of grain at them and said, "If only you could take the husks off this wheat you would be doing something useful indeed."[8]

The boys thought about the problem and went to work on a solution. They discovered that they could remove the husks with a small brush, but doing them all by hand took a long time. After scrounging around the mill, they found an old vat with a rotating paddle wheel inside. The boys lined the vat's walls with rough, brushlike material. Now when they dropped grain inside, the paddles pushed the grain against the walls, which loosened away the husks. Years later, Bell said, "It was a proud day for us when we boys marched into Mr. Herdman's office, presented him with our sample of cleaned wheat, and suggested paddling the wheat."[9]

The process of building the machine, coupled with the pride he experienced when it worked, gave Aleck great satisfaction. It was the necessary first taste of success that he would later remember as he struggled to make the telephone a workable reality.

Aleck's next project was his first experiment with speech, and it involved the family pet. He was curious about why the dog, a small black Skye terrier named Mr. Perd, could not speak.

His father teased him at first and told his son that the dog did not speak because he had no need to. When Aleck persisted with his questions, Melville Bell realized that the boy seriously wondered why the dog could not form words when it growled. Aleck's father suggested that Aleck work on an experiment to explain why the dog could not speak.

Melville told Aleck to teach the dog to growl for a treat. When the dog had mastered this command, Aleck's father showed him how to move Mr. Perd's

THE FAMILY DOG TEACHES SPEECH

When Bell trained his dog to growl on command and then manipulated the dog's lips, he could almost make the growls sound like words. This excerpt is taken from Edwin S. Grosvenor's book, Alexander Graham Bell.

"'The fame of the dog spread,' Bell recalled. 'Many were the visitors who came to the house to see this dog sit up on his hind legs, and with a little assistance from my hand growl forth the words, "How are you, Grand-mama?"' The dog appeared to enjoy the applause and afterward would sit up and growl again, trying to do the performance alone, without his master. Creating a canine conversationalist may seem to be an amusing adolescent diversion, but behind it was a grownup intent: to study the mechanism of sound production and push for new possibilities in communication."

lips so that the dog could form different sounds similar to the "ah" and "oh" sounds of human speech. Melville then told Aleck that he could muffle Mr. Perd's growls by applying slight pressure to the dog's throat, which blocked a steady flow of air.

Although Aleck thought that he was teaching Mr. Perd how to speak, Aleck's father had taught his son the importance of experimentation to test a theory. It was a lesson he understood earlier from the wheat-husk removal machine and believed in again after completing the experiment with Mr. Perd. The experiment also ignited a desire to discover as much as possible about voice manipulation and sound.

Aleck knew that he wanted to learn more about the whole physical process of speech. He also wanted to learn more about his grandfather's theories involving speech. Until this time, Aleck had only seen his grandfather a few times, although the family members stayed in touch with letters. After turning thirteen, he decided to travel to London to study with his grandfather.

STUDYING SOUND WITH THE ORIGINAL BELL ELOCUTIONIST

Aleck's grandfather, the first Alexander Bell, began the family's interest in and involvement with proper speech and oratory presentation. When he was younger, Aleck's grandfather had dreamed of becoming an actor. At the time, however, acting was not considered a favorable occupation by the upper class of society. Since Bell had married into a wealthy family, he could not pursue his acting dreams. He moved instead to London and became a teacher of proper speaking, earning a respectable living by giving speech lessons and lectures. He helped people who stammered, talked with a lisp, or had speech defects.

Following Aleck's successful voice manipulation experiment, he also grew interested in the techniques involved in teaching speech. Aleck wrote about his desire to follow in his grandfather's footsteps in a poem dedicated to the elder Bell:

I am thirteen years, I find;

Your birthday and mine are the same.

I want to inherit your mind,

As well as your much honored name.[10]

It took quite a bit of time for his grandfather to send for Aleck, but in 1862 the third Alexander Bell traveled to London. He would spend a year with the first Alexander Bell, who soon discovered that his namesake was lacking in what he considered a thorough education, saying, "If he wants to inherit my mind, we must do something drastic about this."[11]

Aleck's grandfather immediately immersed Aleck in reading books and made him recite passages from a great many of Shakespeare's plays. The elder and younger Bell often walked to the library in Harrington Square to replenish Aleck's reading material. It was during one of their many trips to the library that Aleck found an article titled "Principles of the Science of Tuning Instruments with Fixed Tones."

The article explained how tuning forks could reproduce certain sounds, and Aleck wondered whether these musical tones could be assigned to the human voice. Many of the principles outlined in the article matched ideas that Aleck had been contemplating regarding sound reproduction. What he learned in that one article would become the backbone of his later experiments with the human voice and with the early telephone.

When he was not studying his new interest in voice reproduction, Aleck attended his grandfather's lectures and classes about proper elocution. He also enjoyed listening to his grandfather perform readings from Charles Dickens and other authors.

When Aleck's father paid one of his many visits to London, Melville Bell took his son to a workshop offered by electrical expert Sir Charles Wheatstone. Through his son's letters, Melville knew that Aleck was intrigued with the idea of reproducing sound and perhaps even the human voice. He believed that Wheatstone's demonstration would further pique Aleck's interest.

Wheatstone had made a machine that could mimic the human voice. The invention intrigued Melville Bell, too, who wondered if the invention might have a practical use as a teaching tool. The demonstration by Wheatstone mesmerized both father and son, and Bell later wrote, "I saw Sir Charles manipulate the machine and heard it speak, and although the articulation was disappointingly crude, it made a great impression on me."[12]

Wheatstone's demonstration, coupled with Aleck's experiences in London, served as major turning points in Aleck's life. Under the guidance of his grandfather, Aleck developed into a determined young man interested in learning more about sound. Much later, he shared these thoughts about that time of his young life and his adventures with the grandfather who nurtured his interests in sound and speech: "This period of my life seems the turning point of my whole career. It converted me from a boy somewhat prematurely into a man."[13]

With the exception of the uncomfortable, fancy clothes that his grandfather insisted he wear, Aleck enjoyed living and learning with his grandfather. The arrangement allowed him the freedom to travel and to research his own interests in sound, and when his time in England drew to a close, he actually dreaded returning to Edinburgh. Aleck knew that he would have to discontinue studying topics of his choice and would have to return to his struggles with learning Latin and Greek.

BECOMING A YOUNG MAN

Later in life, Bell said that the year he had spent with his grandfather in London had helped him gain an attitude of self-confidence and maturity. Biographer Ernest V. Heyn, in his book Fire of Genius, *gives specific examples of that year in London.*

"In 1862, the fifteen-year-old inventor made a move that he later described as 'the turning point of my life.' Leaving school after only four years . . . he joined his grandfather in London. Alexander Bell, seventy-two, was still teaching speech and elocution, a practice he immediately extended to young Aleck, whose declamatory gifts he burnished with joint readings from Shakespeare. He insisted also on transforming the adolescent's dress. Soon Aleck was turned out in full London gentleman's regalia, including kid gloves, top hat, and cane. Though he chafed somewhat at the restrictions of town life in London, his exposure to the magnificent old man gave him a new sense of independence and a seriousness of purpose he had never felt before. When he returned home after a year's visit, he had been 'converted . . . from a boy somewhat prematurely into a man.'"

Alexander Graham Bell

Aleck found it difficult to keep his mind from wondering about sound, tuning instruments, and speech mimicking. He found himself aching to break away from traditional studies to pursue his family's passion for sound and his own growing interest in it.

EXPERIMENTING WITH SOUND AND THE SPEAKING MACHINE

Even after Aleck left his grandfather and returned to Scotland, he continued to study the physical process of speech. Aleck knew that he wanted to choose a course of education that would help him learn more about sound and possibly its reproduction.

As Aleck settled back into his family's routine in Edinburgh, he did not appreciate the rules that his father placed on his time and education. After Aleck had been given the privilege of learning from his grandfather's rich and varied education, he had trouble accepting his father's strict schedule of study.

Melville Bell differed from the elder Alexander Bell in his views of education. He did not believe in allowing young Aleck to travel with him or sit in on his teaching sessions. Melville believed in a more structured education that included attending school and doing homework.

Aleck's father also knew that his son needed a solid foundation in Latin and Greek since so many scientific words are derived from those languages. Likewise, Aleck would need a stronger grasp of some of the sciences if he hoped to ac-

Melville Bell supported his son's interests and ideas.

complish his dream of reproducing human speech.

Melville Bell eventually worked out an idea that would combine his idea of solid homework with Aleck's need to be creative with his studies. He captured both Aleck's and Melly's interest by challenging his sons to build a speaking machine similar to the one he and Aleck had seen in London. Melville believed that the process could qualify as homework since he knew his sons would have to learn necessary details about the vocal process if they worked on such a machine.

The experimentation that Bell, seen here with an early version of the telephone, and his brother conducted early in life led to later ground-breaking inventions.

Aleck was immediately excited. This was exactly the kind of research he needed for learning a hands-on, in-depth understanding of the exact process of human speech. The task was quite complicated because it required the construction of various items that functioned in the same manner as the human organs used for speaking.

For example, the brothers built a model of a throat out of tin. They then used rubber to construct a larnyx, jaws, teeth, pharnyx, nasal cavities, lips, and cheeks. For the palate, they again used rubber, but they also stuffed it with cotton. To simulate the tongue, the brothers shaped a piece of wood to look like a tongue and then covered it in rubber. They then divided the "tongue" into six segments that could be operated with levers. This manipulation would mimic the movements that a human tongue made to produce certain sounds naturally.

The brothers worked hard at building their model, then manipulating the levers, and adjusting the construction when necessary. Sounds eventually came out of the machine when they blew air into it, just as if lungs were pushing air through the vocal organs of a human. Bell later recalled how he and his brother worked together on the project: "My brother Melville [Melly] and I attacked the problem together, and divided up the work. He undertook to make the lungs and the apparatus while I made the tongue and mouth."[14]

This practical study of the human vocal system and the actual construction of the machine provided Aleck with a few mature insights. First, he learned to appreciate science in its interwoven forms, such as the process of human speech and experiments to mimic that process. He knew that he needed to learn more about the human vocal process to pursue his dream of reproducing speech. And he also realized that he would need to learn more about mechanical engineering to put his theory about reproducing speech into workable inventions.

As with all inventors, Aleck and Melly found that some days were filled with progress and others were full of setbacks. They never gave up, though, and at last their apparatus emitted a rough sound.

The brothers tried the word *mamma,* and the machine groaned "Mamma, mamma." As a joke, they placed their machine outdoors where the whole neighborhood could hear it but could not see them. Bell later recalled what happened that day:

> It really sounded like a baby in distress. "Mamma, Mamma" came forth with heart-rendering effect. We heard someone above say, "Good gracious, what can be the matter with that baby," and then footsteps were heard. This, of course, was just what we wanted. We quietly slipped into our house, and closed the door, leaving our neighbors to pursue their fruitless quest for the baby. Our triumph and happiness were complete.[15]

This was the second time that Aleck had built a workable machine. Now he was becoming more comfortable with the process of trial and error involved with inventing. In addition, Bell had become more familiar with the physical process of speaking that aided his later work with the telephone:

Many times were we discouraged and disheartened over our efforts and ready to give the whole thing up in disgust. . . . The making of this talking-machine certainly marked an important point in my career. It made me familiar with the functions of the vocal cords, and started me along the path that led to the telephone.[16]

The success of Aleck's and Melly's speaking machine did not compensate for the suffocation that Aleck felt in his father's home. Aleck was deeply bothered by his father's constant reprimands and criticism regarding his poor grades. At one point, Aleck and Melly even went so far as to pack their bags, planning to run away to one of the unsettled British colonies.

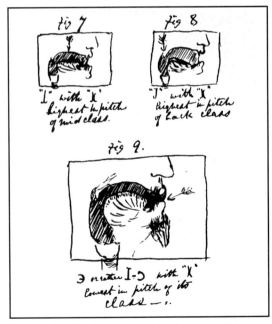

A page from Bell's notebook depicts one of his experiments with sound.

Alexander and his brother, Melville, successfully developed a speaking machine despite many setbacks.

They did not have to run away, however, because a teaching opportunity soon offered escape. Aleck would be able to use all of the education that he had received at his grandfather's side, as well as through his experiments with speech, when he and Melly became teachers. And the process would open a new world for Aleck.

2 A Love for Teaching

As Bell matured into a young man, he continued to discover new things about himself and his dreams. He realized that he enjoyed teaching proper speech as much as his father and grandfather loved their careers as elocutionists. He also knew that he would need to research details about the human voice, as well as all aspects of sound reproduction, if he hoped to make his dream of reproducing human speech a reality.

YOUNG TEACHER

While reading a local paper, Aleck and Melly noticed an advertisement seeking music and elocution teachers at nearby Weston House Academy in Elgin. During this time, it was not unusual for young men to teach at a high school in exchange for credit toward tuition at a local university. But Aleck and Melly had a problem: Neither brother was really old enough to teach since Aleck was barely sixteen and Melly was only two years older. The advertisement also stated that applicants would need to provide a reference. On an impulse, the brothers de-

cided not to mention their ages and to use their father's name as a reference. They wrote a letter to the school's headmaster and did not tell anyone that they had signed Melville Bell's name to it.

The reply from Weston House Academy was addressed to Melville Bell since the school assumed that he had written the letter. Needless to say, he was quite surprised when he opened the acceptance letter from Mr. Skinner, the headmaster of Weston House. He was also furious with his sons' dishonesty and scolded them: "What do you mean by playing a trick like this? What will Mr. Skinner think of us? You ought to know better! Teach Music and Elocution! The idea!"[17]

In time, their father's anger cooled. Trading off teaching with attending classes was a beneficial system that many students took advantage of in Scotland at the time. Melville Bell mulled over the benefits that such a system might present to his sons. He wondered if the responsibility of teaching would finally convince Aleck to work harder in his own classes. At last, Melville Bell consented; but he did so on the condition that Aleck promise to

The Bells pose with family friends in front of their summer home in Manchester-by-the-sea.

apply himself when studying his Latin and Greek courses.

Aleck readily agreed to his father's condition. It was decided that Aleck would teach while Melly attended the University of Edinburgh. They later switched, and Aleck went to the university while Melly taught at Weston House. Since the University of Edinburgh was close to Elgin, it was no trouble at all for the brothers to trade off their teaching and studying. They continued this pattern for the next few years until both Aleck and Melly had received all of the courses they needed to graduate.

Finally, Aleck had studied enough Latin and Greek to help his speech and elocution career for years to come. Even so, he did not enjoy the process and commented years later that he had enough Latin and Greek

> stuffed down my throat to have been of inestimable value to me in understanding the Etymology of the Eng-

lish language, and in giving me a key to the barbarous language of science in which the terms are largely of classical origin.[18]

In 1865, when Aleck was eighteen, his grandfather died and Melville Bell had to make a decision. He pondered whether to stay in Edinburgh, where he had his own following of students, or to move to London and take over his father's elocution practice. After a short time passed, Melville packed Eliza and their youngest son, Edward, and moved to London, where he took over his father's clients and lecture schedule.

YOUNG RESEARCHER

Despite the distance between Melville Bell in London and his oldest sons in Scotland, the three men continued their discussions about speech. During frequent visits and through letters,

VISIBLE SPEECH

Alexander Melville Bell's creation of visible speech was a revolutionary concept used to help deaf people communicate in the mid-1850s. Thomas B. Costain, in his book The Chord of Steel, *puts visible speech into an impacting perspective, which gives a thorough insight into why A. Graham Bell later used the technique in his own teaching.*

"Visible Speech was a concrete method of enabling the dumb [mute] to teach themselves how to speak. To Alexander Melville Bell it was evident that deaf mutes were silent, not because they lacked the physical organ used in speaking, but because they could not hear. . . . But by learning the symbols they could acquire the faculty of making the sounds designated; and from this, in time, would come the ability to speak. As the organ of speech was the same in all people and the action was the same in all mouths, the symbols were universal. They meant the same to a Chinese child unable to ask for rice or a Bantu crone in an African kraal as to a deficient child in a sheltered English home."

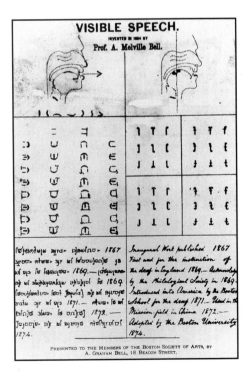

Bell's father created visible speech, a universal alphabet which reduced all human utterances into a series of written symbols.

Melville kept his sons up to date on his latest theories and practices. Many of these discussions concerned a teaching system that Melville had invented called visible speech.

Visible speech involved a series of symbols and pictures that showed the entire vocal process of pronouncing sounds. For example, each vowel sound was assigned a symbol. The symbol was coupled with a picture that gave a detailed illustration of what parts of the vocal system were used to make that vowel sound.

Melville Bell was very successful using this system to help his students learn proper positioning of their tongues and lips to make certain sounds. This system proved especially helpful to deaf children, who were not usually taught to speak since they could not hear to imitate the sound. Visible speech allowed people with hearing impairments to "see" how a sound should be vocalized.

On a visit to London when Aleck was eighteen, he and his father talked in-depth about vowel sounds. They discussed whether those sounds should be considered the primary basis for human speech. Aleck wondered if vowel sounds were a single pitch or a compound pitch. In other words, he wanted to know if the sounds were made up of one pure tone or several.

Remembering the article that he had read in London about tuning instruments and fixed tones, he wondered if human speech could be assigned different tones. Because he had learned the benefits of experimentation, he chose to scientifically solve this question. His curiosity about tone and human speech later proved essential when he chose the components for building the telephone.

After the discussion with his father, Aleck experimented with pitches made by the human tongue. He matched those sounds to different pitches made by tuning forks. Aleck also knew that human speech created vibrations in air. To measure those vibrations, he made a device using stretched membranes that moved when the airwaves hit them.

The membranes would be crucial to the first telephone devices. Later in life, Bell commented on the importance of the membranes and those early experiments: "These experiments paved the way for the appearance of the first membrane telephone, the ancestor of all the telephones."[19]

His follow-up experiments substantiated his theories, and he wrote about the discovery in a report to his father. Aleck's report stated that vowel sounds are formed when the changing volumes of air vibrate and make different pitches. The number of vibrations proved that vowel sounds make several tones. They were compound, not one pure tone. He compared the idea to blowing air across the mouths of bottles that had been filled to different levels. In the conclusion of his report, he stated that vowel sounds were indeed compound, which was a fact not widely known at the time.

YOUNG COLLEAGUE

Based on the solid information in his son's report, Melville Bell suggested that Aleck submit the report to Alexander John Ellis.

COMBINED PATH TO THE TELEPHONE

Many ideas from many inventors helped Bell succeed with his talking telephone. The Book of Knowledge: The Children's Encyclopedia, *edited by Holland Thompson and Arthur Mee, gives a brief listing of some of these other inventors.*

"The boy [Charles Wheatstone] who experimented with the pennies and made an electric battery, and later made a violin play itself, was of a very practical turn of mind. . . . His chief fame depends on the invention of what is called the five-needle telegraph. Yet, he may be said to have started the experiments in the transmission of sound which led to the coming of the telephone.

A great step forward was taken in 1860 by Professor Philip Reis, of Friedrichsdorf, who discovered a principle of transmission which was eventually developed into the modern telephone."

Philip Reis, a poor German schoolteacher, created a telephone that transmitted crude sounds more than a decade before Bell. His invention, however, was largely ignored.

Ellis was a well-known philologist, an expert in the field of linguistics and phonetics.

After studying the report and experiment notes, Ellis recognized Bell's talent and deductive thinking capabilities. Unfortunately, most of Bell's research into vowel sounds had already been conducted and proven by the German scientist Hermann von Helmholtz.

Still, Ellis told Bell to continue with his research for reproducing human speech. In addition to encouraging Bell, Ellis loaned him his own copy of Helmholtz's book describing how tuning forks were used in the German scientist's work. Since the book was written in German, Ellis tried to summarize Helmholtz's conclusion for Bell: "Intermitting electro-magnet streams are produced by the vibration of a tuning fork. . . . Thus [they are] communicated to other forks."[20]

Bell knew that the "sending" tuning forks made a vibration that caused a continuous tone. He mistakenly also believed that the electromagnet streams attached to the sending tuning forks carried that tone by using an electrical current. In reality, the tones were carried on airwaves, much like human ears receive tones when listening to any sound.

It was this mistake about the electrical connection that triggered Bell's imagination and set him on the path to the telephone. He wondered if vibrating tones could be transmitted to a second set of "receiving" tuning forks that were also hooked up to a separate electromagnet. Bell believed that when the tuning forks received the vibration, they would then reproduce the original tone.

This theory was the first time that Bell had added electricity to his

dream of building an apparatus that could send and receive human speech vibrations. It was also the first time that Bell realized that such a machine could forever change the world of communication. This invention Bell dreamed of could quite possibly surpass the only source of instant long-distance communication at the time: the telegraph.

A Talking Telegraph?

The telegraph had always intrigued Bell. Telegraph communication involved an

Claude Chappe, a Frenchman who died in 1805, invented the telegraph in 1791 and was instrumental in the quest for convenient long-distance communication.

operator using a metal lever on his telegraph machine to send an electrical current. The current traveled across electrical lines to a receiving telegraph machine.

The telegraph machines worked on an electrical "make-or-break" system. The make-or-break system occurred when the sending operator pushed down on a metal lever, "making" the electrical current, and when the lever was lifted from the metal base, "breaking" the current. Morse code dots and dashes were assigned to the various lengths of time that the connection was made or broken. The dots and dashes represented letters of the alphabet, and the receiving operator translated them into words and sentences.

Bell sought to invent a similar system and alphabet code for the human speech machine he intended to invent. One person who gave him a great amount of help was the man whose speaking machine Bell had seen years before in London. Sir Charles Wheatstone's most recent success was helping to design the underground telegraph cables that had just been laid beneath the Atlantic Ocean. Bell realized that he and Wheatstone shared not only a love of sound but also an interest in expanding the world's communication.

Bell sought out a chance to speak in person with the famous scientist. He hoped it would be the perfect chance to share his ideas for an apparatus that could surpass the current system of telegraph communication. Wheatstone was impressed by Bell's similar passion for sound. He gave the young man a great

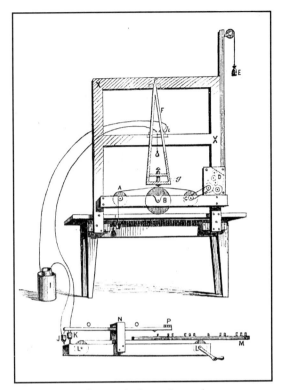

A blueprint of Morse's first telegraph.

deal of attention and listened to all of Bell's questions.

Their discussions lasted a long time, and Wheatstone encouraged Bell to keep searching for ways to fulfill his dream of inventing a so-called talking telegraph. Years later Bell reflected on his visit with Wheatstone: "I came to believe firmly in the feasibility of the telegraphic transmission of speech, and I used to tell my friends that some day we should talk by telegraph."[21]

Bell's enthusiasm was understandable. Transporting spoken words over an electrical current was not yet possible. Anyone who could accomplish such a feat would be a respected hero of communication. If

Before the telephone, quick communication was possible only through the use of the telegraph, which used lines that stretched from coast to coast.

SICKNESS AND TRAGEDY

As a young man, Bell experienced many headaches and had trouble sleeping. His younger brother also suffered with similar occurrences of poor health, and in 1867, when he was only eighteen, Edward died from tuberculosis. The disease was one of the most common sicknesses at the time, and many people died from it. Medical experts believe that tuberculosis is passed from person to person by breathing infected air or by eating infected food. The unsanitary conditions in big cities at the time aided the spread of the disease.

After Edward's death, Bell's parents worried that they might lose him to poor health also.

He decided that it would be better to leave Scotland and move closer to his parents, who were still living in London, England. Bell accepted a teaching position in Bath, a small town only a hundred miles from London.

Although Bell was not as far away from his parents in Bath as he was when he lived in Edinburgh, his mother still worried that he would become sick while living on his own. When she wrote to him, she often relayed her concern over his independence:

Young birds are very prone to try the strength of their wings too soon. The

Bell's theory could be proven with a working apparatus, he believed that he would become a permanent part of communication history.

Although he finally had most of the education and experience he needed to research his ideas, Bell still lacked one important bit of knowledge. He could not invent a machine for reproducing human speech using electricity until he learned more about electricity. Unfortunately, Bell lacked time to study all he needed to learn. To make matters worse, his health was failing.

parent birds know best the proper time for independent flying. You should not have your mind distracted by the care of earning your bread.[22]

Eliza Bell sent her son many letters while he lived in Bath. In addition to expressing her feelings about Bell's health, she also wrote encouraging words about his teaching and his research for the talking telegraph. Eliza also kept him up to date with what Parliament had to say about telegraphic communications with foreign countries. Likewise, she sent him a copy of a new publication titled *World of Science*, which reported on new discoveries that had to do with electricity.

Eliza Bell was interested in her son's ideas, but as a mother, her main concern centered on his health. She worried that as he worked hard to make a success of his new teaching position, he would continue to have headaches and not sleep well. The letters between mother and son became a constant tug-of-war, with Eliza stressing her desire for Bell to move home. Bell did not help matters when he often mentioned how tired he felt and how much weight he had lost.

YOUNG TEACHER

After only a year in Bath, Bell gave in to his mother's wishes and moved to London. He decided to rest and to help his father with his elocution practice by tutoring students when he had the strength. He brought with him a glowing letter from the principal of the school in

Bath, which complimented Bell on his "talent for communicating his knowledge in such a way as to secure and sustain the interest of his pupils. I have never seen English reading taught with greater success."[23]

While living with his parents, Bell regained a little of his strength and began teaching deaf children using the visible speech system. The school where he taught was run by one of Melville Bell's pupils, Susanna E. Hull, and through this class, Bell discovered something surprising about himself.

Even though he still dreamed of building a talking telegraph, he felt a special joy as he helped deaf children learn to speak. The children caught on quickly to the idea of visible speech and then learned to speak by using the pictures as their guides. Being a part of their success brought Bell a great deal of satisfaction.

Bell was troubled, however, by the fact that deaf children were segregated from hearing children. Because these children could learn to speak, Bell believed that they should interact and communicate with hearing children. It was a belief not widely accepted at the time, and it became an issue that Bell would defend again and again in his long life. The common practice was to keep all deaf children separated in schools and to have them communicate by sign language, an alphabet of symbols made by hand gestures.

Hull agreed with Bell, asserting that deaf children should learn to speak and read lips. When the British government decided to support more modern approaches to teaching deaf children, Hull wrote to Bell. She hoped that he would support her ideas about visible speech and lipreading:

> It is of utmost importance that our legislators should be drawn to adopt the best method of instruction. With some modifications, no doubt Articulation and Lip-reading is by far the most successful plan.[24]

Articulation was Hull's term for the visible speech system that Bell had introduced to her students. Likewise, through lip-reading, deaf children could learn to watch the movements of a speaker's lips and interpret what that person was saying. When lipreading and visible speech were taught together, children learned a method of communicating with all people, not just those who knew sign language.

As Bell became more committed to making a difference in these children's lives, he spent more time at the school. Once again his health suffered, and he became weaker. His parents worried about his continued weight loss and pale appearance. As a result, they considered moving him away from London, with its polluted air and disease-ridden streets.

Melville Bell's relocation thoughts centered around Canada, a country that he had once visited while lecturing about his visible speech technique. There were no large cities in the area of Canada that he was considering, and the air was much cleaner.

Before he could decide, however, tragedy struck again. In 1870, at the age of twenty-five, Melly also died from tuberculosis. Even though Melly had stayed in Edinburgh when his brother moved to England, he and Aleck had remained close through letters. They had also continued to share their ideas about speech and sound, just as they had done as young teenagers. The brothers had even hoped to someday teach together, but those dreams ended with Melly's death.

With only one son left in the family, Eliza and Melville decided to make the move they had been discussing. They sold their

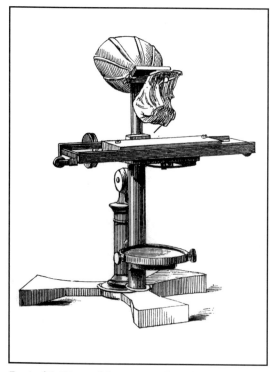

Part of Bell's teaching centered on the use of such inventions as the phonautograph, which showed students the shape of sound vibrations and guided them in recreating a sound.

Because of Bell's poor health, he decided to follow his parents when they moved to Canada. Despite his worry that he was moving to an uncivilized country, he eventually lived in this house in Nova Scotia with his wife and children.

house and many of their belongings, and they strongly encouraged Aleck to join them as they crossed the Atlantic Ocean to live and work in Canada.

One biographer summarizes Bell's grief for Melly as he wrote to his parents about making the move or staying in London. Eliza's response is also included:

> "I collected all the things that were to be kept, into the study—*and locked myself in*—and tried to imagine myself in the Backwoods of Canada," he wrote them. "It was not very hard to imagine . . . sitting on borrowed chairs—in the empty classroom." His mother sought to reassure him. "You don't really think

you are going to the backwoods, do you?" she wrote back. "You are merely going into a country house, and will have civilized society there, just as much as you have here." In that society, Aleck would seek and finally find his fame and fortune.[25]

It was a tough choice. He had friends and colleagues whom he had grown fond of during his teaching years. Still, he knew that his health was poor, so he followed his parents. Bell hoped he might regain enough strength to return to teaching and to researching his ideas for reproducing speech so that he could begin working on a talking telegraph.

3 Respected Teacher and Researcher

In 1870, during the ocean voyage to Canada, Alexander Graham Bell worried that he might not grow strong enough to become a respected teacher as he had been back in England. His six-foot-tall body was thin, and his dark hair contrasted greatly against his pasty skin. He also worried that he might not ever fulfill his dreams for reproducing speech, but his most pressing concerns revolved around regaining his health so that he could return to teaching.

A NEW HOME

The voyage to Canada was long and tiring. By August, when his ship reached the waters north of Nova Scotia and turned into the Gulf of St. Lawrence, Bell was ready to land. As he stood on deck, looking toward the wooded shores of Canada, he breathed in cool fresh air and felt a strong fondness for the majestic landscape. One biographer captures Bell's feelings as the ship moved closer to the city of Quebec:

It was an experience never to be forgotten. The immensity and majesty of the panorama moved him as nothing had ever moved him before, and at the same time it exhilarated him and made it hard for him, impulsive and active as he was, to remain still.[26]

After leaving the ship, the family endured another few days of traveling across rugged country before finally settling in Brantford, Ontario, along the Grand River. The air was crisp and clear, and large polluted cities were far from the family's home. The area reminded Bell of his native Scotland and seemed to help rebuild his strength.

Most of Bell's first weeks in Brantford were spent resting and thinking. At a grouping of birch trees located at the edge of their property and close to the river, Bell hung a hammock between two of the trees. During that initial summer, and for many years to come, that hammock in the birches was Bell's favorite thinking spot. Toward the end of his life he said that many of his early conceptual problems with the telephone were worked out when he visited his parents' home and stretched out on his hammock.

As winter approached, Bell's health showed great improvement. He felt strengthened, his color returned to normal, and his eagerness to begin teaching again occupied his thoughts. He also wanted to get busy experimenting with the reproduction of human speech.

While his son had been resting, Melville Bell had begun traveling and lecturing about the visible speech system. In the spring of 1871, Melville began touring New England and demonstrating his revolutionary system. While in Boston, he met Sarah Fuller, the headmistress of the Boston School for the Deaf.

Fuller was greatly impressed with the visible speech system and asked Melville Bell if he would teach it in her school on a regular basis. Bell declined the offer but told Fuller that he had a son who was a gifted teacher of visible speech, and offered to send Aleck to Boston if she would promise to keep an eye on his health. Upon Melville's return to Brantford, he shared with his family his discussion with Fuller and her need for an instructor:

> I told her that I had spent twenty years in devising the system, and now I didn't wish to teach it, but that I had a son who could come to Boston if it seemed advisable to take the risk of affecting his health by the change in climate. Miss Fuller told me that whatever she could do to care for and protect my son's health would gladly be done.[27]

Alexander Graham Bell was thrilled with the idea of teaching again, and he prepared to leave immediately. On April

Bell (top right) and his colleagues stand with students outside the Pemberton School for the Deaf, in Boston, 1871.

5, 1871, Bell traveled to Boston to meet with Sarah Fuller and learn more about the school. During his visit, he went into the classrooms with her and worked with the children. Bell's manner was gentle, and the children responded well to his method of instruction. Fuller immediately recognized his talents and hired him on the spot.

Fuller was Bell's supervisor, and he respected her as a fellow professional. He also admired her compassionate nature, and she soon became a trusted friend. Later that month, when he wrote to his parents about his first few days in Boston and about meeting Sarah Fuller, he said, "I never saw *love, goodness,* and *firmness* so blended in one face before. Her abilities

FIRST IMPRESSIONS OF BOSTON'S SCHOOL FOR THE DEAF

Bell's keen sense of observation comes out in this letter to his parents during the early part of April 1871. Excerpted from the Alexander Graham Bell Family Papers, *a part of the Library of Congress's on-line American Memory Collection, this letter gives detailed descriptions of the teachers at the Boston School for the Deaf, where he had agreed to teach.*

"The Principal is Miss Fuller—a 'young lady' (I compliment her by the epithet) who seems particularly qualified for her position. I never saw Love, Goodness, and Firmness so blended in one face before. . . .

Miss True I can't say I am in love with. . . . She seems to have a far higher opinion of herself than any one else has . . . . I don't like her manner with the children either. She seems to always be out of patience with one of them. . . .

Miss Bond—I should think is the oldest of the four. I don't know whether to like her or not. I am rather inclined to the former. She is by no means pretty and wears specs. . . .

Miss Barton, I suppose is the one Papa warned me of (?!!) for she does rather incline towards prettiness. She is a Miss Fuller with more animation about her. Evidently has her whole heart in the children. I should think she has a very high opinion of her own powers, at the same time seems to have very good natured abilities. I think she is the best teacher of the four. She manages her class with the firmness of a man, and is never out of temper with the children. Miss Fuller I think most of however. Her abilities seem very great, but she is very modest about them, and she is overflowing with genuine goodness towards the children."

are very great, and she is overflowing with genuine goodness toward the children."[28]

In keeping her pledge to care for Melville Bell's son, Fuller arranged for her new teacher to stay at a nearby boardinghouse. She and her sister also opened their own homes to Bell for dinners and visits. Their generosity made it quite easy for Bell to fall into a pattern of teaching during the day and enjoying stimulating conversation with Fuller during the evenings. He shared with her his ideas about reproducing speech by someday building a talking telegraph, and she encouraged him to pursue his research.

Bell's ability to help deaf children learn to speak using the visible speech system brought him personal satisfaction, but it also won him praise and respect. In 1871 the School Committee of the City of Boston stated in a report:

> Perhaps nothing has contributed so much during the year to the value of the instruction in this school as the introduction of Prof. Alex. Melville Bell's system of "visible speech" which was done by his son, Mr. A. G. Bell.[29]

Even as he received praise from his peers and supervisors about his teaching, Bell continued researching his theory for reproducing human speech. During this time, Boston was one of the most scientifically and culturally rich cities in the United States. The city had libraries stocked with the best books and universities staffed by the best professors.

Boston was a great place for Bell to find the resources he needed to begin building the various components to make a talking telegraph. He spent what money he could afford on the different parts for his experiments, and he often worked late into the night on the inventions. Even Fuller was caught up in his enthusiasm. Years later she wrote,

> He often came to our house in the evening and worked on his experiments (he was always experimenting with means to transmit sound) until past midnight—and sometimes until two in the morning! I always sat with him and followed his successes and failures with extreme interest.[30]

One such experiment involved a balloon. During one of their evening conversations, Bell asked Fuller to hold a balloon tightly against her chest. He then made a few loud noises to show her how noises caused vibrations in the air. Those vibrations could be felt through the balloon. Bell wanted Fuller's permission to use balloons in the classroom. By having his students hold balloons to their chests, Bell believed that they would be able to feel, and thus learn to identify, the vibrations of different sounds.

For example, if students learned to identify the vibration that a horse carriage made as it rolled in the street, then they would be alerted to potential danger. Fuller agreed that the balloons could help the children recognize street noises, especially in the dark when their vision was also weak, and she authorized Bell to start using the balloons as teaching tools.

Bell used these discoveries about vibrations to sketch out items for his talking telegraph that might also reproduce vibrations. He looked forward to devoting more time to his ideas and research once he returned home to Brantford at the end of his first semester of teaching.

As it turned out, however, Bell could not make much progress after returning to Brantford because he spent a good deal of his time teaching with his father. Now that his son was old enough to teach, Melville Bell wanted him to accompany him as he gave lectures about visible speech. Summer was soon over, and Aleck returned to Boston to resume teaching at Fuller's school. He also began lecturing about visible speech at other schools for the deaf in the northeastern United States.

Often these schools asked him to teach a class, and Bell was quick to oblige. Before long, he had divided his teaching time between Fuller's school and the Clarke School for the Deaf in Northampton, Massachusetts. Because of Bell's busy

Sketches from Bell's notebook detailing his experiments with the telephone.

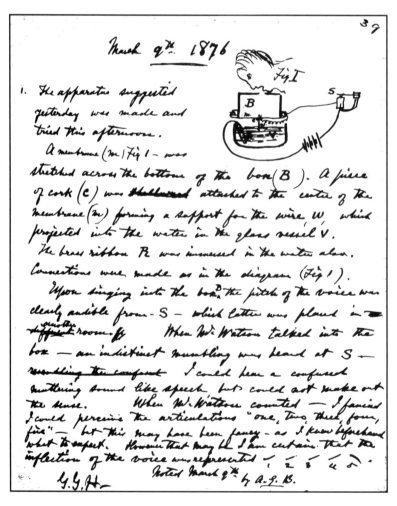

teaching schedule, he had little time to conduct research or work on his experiments. As a result, he wondered how he could lessen his teaching load and increase the amount of time that he could work on his talking telegraph.

TUTORING

As he struggled with different options for squeezing more hours into the day for his experiments, Bell talked over his feelings with Sarah Fuller. He knew that she understood both his desire to teach and his desire to work on his experiments.

Because Fuller considered Bell to be an excellent teacher, she could have encouraged him to forget his experiments and teach only at her school. But she respected him too much to do that. She did encourage him to become more established in Boston, and she suggested that he could tutor deaf students and new teachers about the use of visible speech:

> I urge you to make Boston your place of residence, and advertise a plan for receiving pupils. Either teachers to be trained for work with deaf children, or deaf persons—adults or children. It seems to me that a fixed address will give dignity to your announcement and inspire confidence.[31]

This idea made a great deal of sense to Bell. He could take on the number of students he wished and still have time to work on his experiments. During the hours that he did not have any students,

he could research more about electricity and how he would use it in his inventions.

After looking for and acquiring a location to use as a private school, Bell put the finishing touches on preparing his advertisement. In a brochure dated October 1, 1872, Bell eloquently stated,

> Mr. A. Graham Bell begs to announce the opening of an Establishment for the study of Vocal Physiology; for the correction of Defects in Utterance; and for Practical Instruction in "Visible Speech," the system of Universal Phonetics invented by his father, Professor A. Melville Bell.[32]

Because of Bell's growing fame, he soon had quite a few students enrolled in his school. Georgie Sanders was one of Bell's first pupils. He was the deaf son of Thomas Sanders, a wealthy leather-goods merchant. Since Georgie was only five years old, Bell thought the boy would learn better in his own home, where he would be more comfortable. With Georgie, Bell decided to modify his usual method of teaching visible speech.

Instead of simply showing Georgie a chart of the visible speech alphabet indicating how to pronounce vowel sounds, Bell labeled the youngster's toys with cards. Each card spelled out the object in both the regular alphabet and the visible speech alphabet. This process helped Georgie understand that every object had a name that could be spelled in letters, and those letters had sounds that could be produced with speech.

It was in a workshop like this that Bell experimented and invented.

Another method of tutoring that Bell used with Georgie was wearing a glove that had the letters of the alphabet written on it. Bell showed Georgie specific points, such as at the fingertips and knuckles, where letters matched those on his toys. He would then spell out the name of an object by using the letters on the glove, and Georgie would copy it on his bare hand. Using this system, the boy learned to spell the names of the objects in his room.

It was not long before Georgie could spell anything that he wanted by using the letters positioned on Bell's glove. Both teacher and pupil soon began to spell out words and phrases to "talk" with one another by using the letter positions. This particular method also helped Georgie advance to the next level of communication. Now when they were outdoors—where objects were not labelled with cards or pictures—Bell could still teach Georgie the names by using the glove.

Before long Bell took Georgie outside often, spelling any object that was unfamiliar to the boy. Bell later recalled his satisfaction with the success of the glove after taking Georgie on an outing to a popular museum where they communicated quite well:

The use of the glove was so little noticeable that [soon] I could talk to him freely in a crowd without attracting the attention of others. I took him to Barnum's museum and talked to him all the time the lions were being fed, and I am sure that no one among the spectators had the slightest suspicion that the boy was deaf.[33]

Georgie's father was impressed with his son's progress under Bell's guidance. Because Bell was at the Sanders' house so often, he would often share with Thomas Sanders his ideas for reproducing human speech. Sanders was especially intrigued by Bell's idea to make a machine that could transmit voices by using an electrical current. As a businessman who always kept an eye out for profitable opportunities, Sanders gave serious thought to investing in Bell's idea.

INVESTORS FOR HIS RESEARCH

Sanders believed that Bell's talking telegraph could be one of the greatest inventions ever built. Thus, if he invested his money in Bell's machine, he would receive a great deal of money if the invention was successful. The talking telegraph had the potential to be a great success, too, because at the time the telegraph was still the only system of immediate long-distance communication. If Sanders could help Bell come up with a machine to compete with the telegraph, both history and money could be made.

Bell and Sanders were not the only men who tried to invent a machine to compete with the telegraph. Many prominent and wealthy men were also interested in putting their money behind young inventors and their experiments. A great deal of research and energy by these inventors was devoted to experimenting with telegraph machines that could send more than one message at a time.

The telegraph wires strung across the country were capable of only sending one message at a time, which made telegraphs expensive. Therefore, most telegraph communication was limited to the small percentage of people who could afford it. But if an inventor somehow built a machine that could send more than one message at a time, he would make communication available to many more people because prices would be more affordable. It would also ensure financial success for that inventor and his investors.

Sanders became Bell's first partner when he agreed to finance the experiments. Sanders also encouraged Bell to move into his mother's large home so that the inventor would have more room to spread out his inventions. Bell was allowed to use both the basement and third floor for his research and experiments. As an afterthought and a matter of convenience, Sanders decided to move Georgie to his mother's house as well. He wanted to make Georgie's continued education as easy on Bell as possible.

Bell could not have been happier with the arrangement. It was a perfect setup for this stage of his young adulthood as he worked hard to earn a living while still aiming for his dream. During the day, Bell would leave to teach other pupils; in the afternoons and early evenings, he privately tutored young Georgie. At night he had spare time and

Because the telegraph, shown here in a reenactment, was the only system of immediate long-distance communication, Sanders and Hubbard believed that Bell's talking telegraph could be a great success.

comfortable surroundings to either study or experiment.

Parts for experiments were expensive, however, so when another man showed interest in his work, along with the financial means to support it, Bell welcomed him as a partner, too. Gardiner Greene Hubbard was a patent attorney and businessman who had a deaf daughter named Mabel. Hubbard had known Bell as his daughter's teacher, and over time he became interested in Bell's experiments.

In 1872, following their first meeting, Hubbard often welcomed Bell into his home. He wanted to hear Bell's ideas about teaching deaf people to speak, so he frequently invited Bell to Sunday dinner. During these visits, Bell would also discuss his latest progress with his talking telegraph.

Bell received much more than an additional business partner when he began attending the Hubbard family meals. He enjoyed talking with Gardiner Hubbard, and he often played the piano for Hubbard's wife. He even squatted down on his hands and knees to participate in games with the younger children in the family. Over time, he realized that he especially enjoyed spending time with Mabel. Although Mabel was not much older than sixteen, she intrigued Bell with her gentle manner and her smile. Within a few months of regularly visiting with the Hubbards, Bell realized he was falling in love with the attractive young woman.

Partly because of Mabel's age, and partly because he had so little money, Bell chose to delay telling the Hubbards about his feelings for their daughter. Instead, he waited and continued his discussions with Gardiner Hubbard about inventions and telegraphic communication. One biographer explains that the men's shared interests would prove beneficial to both of their careers:

Hubbard and Bell thus had much in common, and became good friends. Hubbard was a patent attorney specializing in mechanical and electrical invention; he was particularly intrigued by telegraphy.[34]

Like many others at the time, Hubbard believed that the next invention in communication would be a multiple telegraph. He told Bell that he would provide monetary support for the inventions if Bell concentrated his research and experiments on building a multiple telegraph.

Even though Bell would have preferred to work only on a talking telegraph, he needed Hubbard's support

TWO KEY MEN WHO HELPED BELL SUCCEED

Although Bell had the intelligence to invent the telephone, he did not have the money for his experiments. He found two men to fund his work, but they did not readily trust one another. Still, as Edwin S. Grosvenor states in Alexander Graham Bell, *they worked together to make the Bell Telephone Company profitable.*

"An air of mild distrust lingered between Gardiner Hubbard and his other partner, Thomas Sanders. Sanders viewed Hubbard as a promoter, which in 1875 generally referred to someone with loose ethics. Hubbard looked down on Sanders as a merchant albeit with legal skills not clever enough to be trusted with important inventions. In spite of the friction, a mutual dependence held them together, for Hubbard needed Sanders' investment capital, and Sanders needed Hubbard's Washington connections. . . . Once he [Hubbard] was sure that the telephone was a serious practical invention, Hubbard launched the Bell Telephone Company and nursed it through its early years, when the tiny firm had to compete with giant Western Union."

TELLING THE HUBBARDS ABOUT HIS LOVE FOR MABEL

On June 24, 1875, Bell wrote a letter (A. G. Bell Family Papers/Library of Congress) to Mabel Hubbard's mother, proclaiming his love for her daughter. This letter is part of the Alexander Graham Bell Family Papers.

"Dear Mrs. Hubbard:

Pardon me for the liberty I take in addressing you at this time, but I am in deep trouble, and can only go to you for advice.

I have discovered that my interest in my dear pupil—Mabel—has ripened into a far deeper feeling than that of mere friendship. In fact I have learned to love her very sincerely.

It is my desire to let her know now—how dear she is to me, and to ascertain from her own lips what her feeling toward me may be. Of course I cannot tell what favor I may meet within her eyes. But this I do know—that if devotion on my part can make her life any happier—I am willing to give my whole heart to her. . . .

I promise aforehand to abide by your decision however hard it may be for me to do so. Believe me, dear Mrs. Hubbard.

Yours very respectfully,
Graham Bell"

Mabel and Alexander Bell at the family's summer home.

because he was always short of money to spend on parts for his inventions. The meager wages he earned by tutoring were hardly enough to meet his current living expenses. He also knew that it would take a successful invention to earn the money he needed in order to ask Mabel to marry him. One biographer believes that marriage may have been a major incentive for Bell's invention:

> Clearly the market was ripe for telegraphy-related inventions. An abundance of ideas (as well as motives—not the least of which was to earn much-needed money to hasten marriage prospects and independence) pushed Bell into becoming an inventor.[35]

Whatever his incentive, Bell was now able to put more time and effort into inventing. Sanders had given Bell early financial help and plenty of room for his inventions, and Hubbard offered even more money and a specific knowledge about patenting inventions. Bell began researching and experimenting with inventions that he hoped would result in a successful multiple telegraph that would please himself as well as his investors.

4 Inventing the Telephone

Bell's life became more complicated as he devoted more time to his research and experiments. He still taught a few pupils, but as he made progress with his inventions, he realized that the process would take even more time and study.

At this point in his career, Bell faced some tough decisions. His parents wanted him to spend more time teaching because they did not believe inventing would offer their son a stable career. In addition to his parents' negative attitude, Bell realized that he still lacked most of the mechanical and electrical skills he needed to make his inventions work. Solving these problems became a priority.

MEETING THOMAS WATSON

Bell needed to have solidly built working models so that he could demonstrate his scientific drawings and ideas for his financial backers. However, he was not the most talented man when it came to building models. To solve this problem, Bell sought the aid of a reliable workshop in Boston owned by Charles Williams. At this shop was a young machinist named Thomas Watson, who would later be-

come Bell's greatest assistant with the telephone. Watson later recalled his first impression of Bell:

> In the early of winter 1874 I was making . . . some experimental exploding torpedo apparatus. That apparatus will always be connected in my mind with the telephone, for one day when I was hard at work on it, a tall slender, quick-motioned man with a pale face, black side whiskers, and a drooping big nose and high sloping forehead crowned with bushy, jet black hair, came rushing out of the office and over to my work bench.[36]

Before long, Watson would become just as impressed with Bell's ideas as he had been with Bell's physical appearance. The two men were quite interested in each other's capabilities and soon discovered that they worked well together. With Bell's shortcomings remedied by Watson's mechanical ability and electrical knowledge, the two men now faced only one major obstacle: time. They were under a great deal of pressure by Hubbard and Sanders to invent the multiple telegraph before someone else beat them to it.

BUILDING A
MULTIPLE TELEGRAPH

The race to build a multiple telegraph was being run by many talented inventors during the early to mid-1870s. Each of the inventors running this technological race had made certain progress, but many had been stalled by design flaws. The most common flaw was too much static noise on the wire when more than one message was being sent. Because the telegraph lines used only one circuit and the wires were not insulated as they are today, the static noise was not muffled.

Bell's multiple telegraph had a slightly different twist than those of other inventors. Although most inventors chose to copy the electrical system and the Morse code alphabet that telegraphy currently employed, Bell chose instead to use tuning forks. These forks would produce musical tones, which Bell believed would reduce the amount of static on the line.

Remembering what he had read about tuning forks in Helmholtz's book, Bell hoped to transmit different pitches across a single wire. He also planned to employ the make-and-break circuitry system currently used in Morse code. But with Bell's design, the musical tones would be received and unscrambled so that the messages could be translated into letters.

As Bell suspected, the key difference in his machine, was that the musical tones did not cause the static noise that the other multiple telegraphs made. If perfected, Bell's system would allow many messages to be sent across one wire, and it would become the first multiple telegraph. Bell called his machine a harmonic telegraph because of the musical tones it sent.

While building the harmonic telegraph, Bell constantly adjusted his theories and drawings to work out problems in the transmission. Then Watson would adjust the machines to test each new possibility. Because of the stress of working such long hours on the experiments, Bell knew that he would have to also adjust his lifestyle.

Thomas Augustus Watson, a machinist, helped Bell to build prototypes of his ideas.

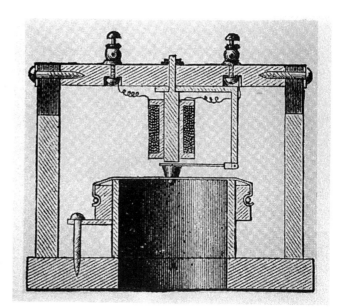

This early telephone transmitted recognizable sounds, but not clear speech. It confirmed Bell's belief in telephony enough for him to write a critical patent for "Improvements in Telegraphy."

He could not teach all day and then spend all night working on his inventions. The longer he kept up the hectic pace, the more irritable and exhausted he became.

Melville and Eliza Bell also feared for their son's health as he spent more time studying and working and less time eating and sleeping. In their letters, they advised their son to continue teaching and to cut back on inventing. Bell understood their concern, but he could not give up his important work—he had investors to please. If he quit inventing, Sanders and Hubbard would consider him a failure and would not invest any more money in his research or inventions.

COMPETITION

Bell decided that his best option would be to quit tutoring and to work only on his experiments. Shortly after making these changes, he recovered some of his strength. Now he believed that he had a chance to compete with his strongest fellow inventors.

One competitor who was close to success with devices similar to Bell's was a man named Elisha Gray. Gray's progress made the time element for discovery much more critical.

In a letter dated May 24, 1875, Bell wrote to his parents informing them of his decision to quit teaching and to devote all of his time to the telegraphy experiments. The letter also gives a glimpse of his concerns about Gray:

> I am so immersed in telegraphy and science that I find it impossible to write freely about anything else. . . . Since I gave up professional work and devoted myself exclusively to telegraphy, I have been steadily gaining health and strength, and am now in a fit state to encounter Mr. Gray or anyone else.[37]

Even though Bell considered Gray a serious competitor regarding the multiple telegraph, Bell could not discipline himself not to work on other inventions at the same time. His bright mind had a habit of wondering about other possible inventions, and he sometimes had trouble sticking with only one project.

Luckily, the spacious rooms of his landlady's house gave him enough separate working areas that he could set up several inventions at once. When frustrated by complications with the harmonic telegraph, Bell would begin tinkering with his favorite apparatus—the talking telegraph that he hoped would one day transmit speech.

Watson's mechanical skills and electrical knowledge had finally made it possible for Bell to edge closer to success on his dream machine. Watson later recalled how Bell shared the idea with him during their first year of working together:

One evening, when we were resting from our struggles with the [telegraphic] apparatus, Bell said to me, "Watson, I want to tell you of another idea. . . . If I could make a current of electricity vary in intensity, precisely as the air varies in density during the production of sound, I should be able to transmit speech telegraphically." He then sketched an instrument that he thought would do this.[38]

The idea of reproducing human speech and transmitting it across wires certainly intrigued Watson, but he knew it would divert their attention away from the multiple telegraph. When Watson chose not to devote any more time to the project, Bell decided to write about his theory instead.

BELIEVING IN THE TELEPHONE

In early 1875 Bell went to New York to meet with Joseph Henry, who was the respected

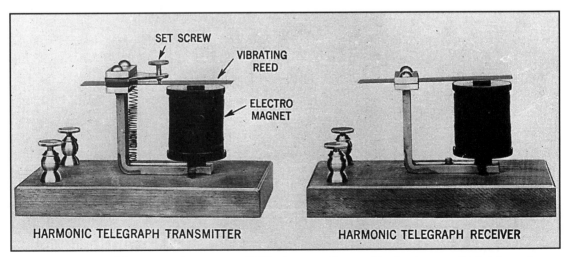

The greatest competition among inventors at Bell's time was the quest to develop a multiple telegraph. Pictured above is Bell's solution, the harmonic telegraph.

director of the Smithsonian Institution. Bell had hoped that the older gentleman could give him some ideas about how to publish his theory of reproducing human speech.

Henry, however, was so impressed by Bell's demonstration of the simple device that he told Bell that he should perfect the invention rather than simply write about it. Likewise, Henry encouraged Bell to acquire the necessary electrical knowledge to make the invention work.

To a man who was working hard and reaping little financial rewards or recognition, this encouragement was exactly what Bell needed. He knew that Watson could help him with the electrical problems, and he had a new burst of excitement for his talking telegraph. Bell was so excited that he wrote to his parents and told them what Henry had shared and the difference his words had made in his life:

> I felt that I had not the electrical knowledge necessary to overcome the difficulties. His laconic answer was, "GET IT." I cannot tell you how much these two words have encouraged me. I live too much in an atmosphere of discouragement for scientific pursuits.[39]

Henry's encouragement prompted Bell to work harder on building a practical talking telegraph. That early telephone that Bell showed to Henry had many of the same components used in the harmonic telegraph.

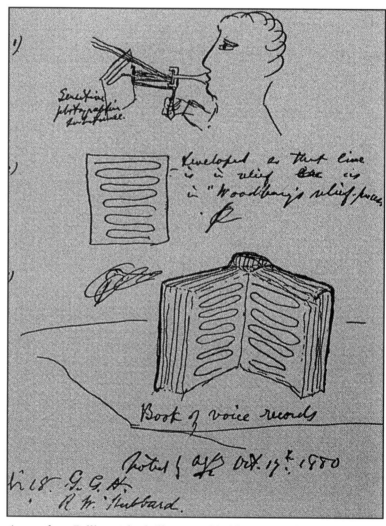

A page from Bell's notebook illustrates his idea to record voice photographically on a light-sensitive medium. This drawing foreshadows Bell's subsequent efforts to improve Edison's phonograph.

The crucial parts of the harmonic telegraph were the steel reeds that stimulated vibrations. Those vibrations could be manipulated to cause the make-or-break flow of electricity. Unfortunately, the steel reeds were troublesome because they often broke. Even though the reeds were unreliable for the make-or-break connection in the harmonic telegraph, their unreliability proved to benefit the invention of the telephone. It was a stuck reed that led Bell to discover how to make a vibrating circuit work for his talking telegraph.

Actors portray Bell and Watson with their first working prototype of the telephone.

FIRST STEPS TO THE TELEPHONE

One day, while Watson was working on the harmonic telegraph by tinkering with a stuck reed, Bell heard the tone from the vibrations of the reed in the next room. The reed fluctuated constantly over the line because it was stuck. Constant fluctuation was something that the men had not yet been able to master electronically in their work on the talking telegraph.

That constant fluctuation reminded Bell of the machine that he and Melly had built to reproduce sound. In that experiment, he had used stretched rubber membranes to carry the constant vibrations caused by speech. Bell immediately went into the other room and tried to explain to Watson that they could use membranes for the talking telegraph.

Watson agreed, and they began spending more of their time and attention on the talking telegraph. They knew that an invention that could reproduce speech had much greater potential to make them successful than a multiple telegraph.

How the Telephone Worked

A few days later Watson and Bell perfected the first working telephone using the membranes along with electromagnets to carry sound waves over an electrical current. The magnets picked up the air vibrations and caused the make-or-break system that was essential to the air vibrations' being reproduced realistically at the receiving end of the apparatus. The sensitive nature of the stretched membranes that were attached at both ends made all the difference in the reliability of the flow.

In June 1875 Bell and Watson constructed the first working telephone. With this device, a person spoke into a hole at the bottom of an apparatus that resembled a wooden box.

At the sending end of the machine, the voice's airwaves struck the stretched membrane. The membrane was attached to one end of a steel reed, which was positioned over an electromagnet. The other end of the steel reed was attached to an electric wire. Tiny vibrations caused by speech were sent over the wire to a receiving electromagnet, attached to another steel reed and membrane, which then vibrated. The vibrations recreated the airwaves that reproduced the original speech.

Although the quality of the sound transmissions was crude, the voices could be understood. More work was necessary to reproduce the effects across a longer distance, but Bell

A page from Bell's patent for the telephone and the harmonic telegraph.

was happy. The working machine proved his lifelong theory that speech could be reproduced and transmitted across wires using electricity.

During the next year, Bell and Watson continued their hectic work schedule. They researched and constructed many types of speaking devices, hoping to make the telephone work consistently and reliably. Each new tinkering brought success closer.

On March 7, 1876, Patent No. 174.465 was issued to Bell. A patent is a document issued by the government that grants a special right of discovery to someone who has invented a new machine or a new improvement to a machine. Patents protect inventors from people who might try to claim that they were the first ones to invent a machine. Patents only protect the inventor in that government's jurisdiction, however, which means inventors need to file patents in each country they choose to claim a right of invention.

Three days after being issued the patent, Bell and Watson were working with a newly constructed liquid transmitter and were prepared to test it. The liquid, which was a better conductor of electricity, replaced the electromagnets that had been used in the earlier versions of the telephone.

1875

THIS MODEL OF BELL'S FIRST TELEPHONE IS A DUPLICATE OF THE INSTRUMENT THROUGH WHICH SPEECH SOUNDS WERE FIRST TRANSMITTED ELECTRICALLY, 1875.

The first telephones used telegraph wires to send messages.

For the test, Bell was in one room with the sending end of the telephone, and Watson was in another room near the receiving end. Watson had no idea what Bell had planned to say when he spoke into his end of the telephone. He was surprised to hear an agitated voice say, "Mr. Watson, come here, I want to see you."[40] Bell had knocked over a flask of acid and his call for help became part of history. Watson came bursting into the room, saying he had heard every word, clearly and distinctly. The test had been a success.

Later that night, Bell wrote to his father about the discovery, stating his belief that this invention would someday be put into use in all houses—a feat the telegraph companies could not do:

Articulate speech was transmitted intelligibly this afternoon. I have constructed a new apparatus operated by the human voice. . . . I feel that I have struck the solution of a great problem—and the day is coming when telegraph wires will be laid on to all houses just like water or gas—and friends will converse with one another without leaving home.[41]

"MR. WATSON—COME HERE—I WANT TO SEE YOU"

March 10, 1876, was the day that the first telephone conversation took place and a day that Bell recorded in his notebook, which is now part of the Alexander Graham Bell Family Papers *at the Library of Congress.*

"The improved instrument shown in Fig. 1 was constructed this morning and tried this evening. P is a brass pipe and W the platinum wire, M the mouth piece and S the armature of the receiving instrument.

Mr. Watson was stationed in one room with the receiving instrument—he pressed one ear closely against S and closed his other ear with his hand. The transmitting instrument was placed in another room and the doors of both rooms were closed.

I then shouted into M the following sentence: 'Mr. Watson—come here—I want to see you.' To my delight he came and declared that he had heard and understood what I said. I asked him to repeat the words. He answered, 'You said, "Mr. Watson—come here—I want to see you."'

We then changed places and I listened at S while Watson read a few passages from a book into the mouth piece M. It was certainly the case that articulate sounds proceeded from S. The effect was loud but indistinct and muffled."

Bell's notebook entry from March 10, 1876, records the first telephone conversation in American history.

Bell's excitement, so obvious in this letter to his father, was also shared by Thomas Sanders. Gardiner Greene Hubbard, however, was not as supportive at first. He still believed that Bell should devote more time to the multiple, or harmonic, telegraph invention instead of to the telephone.

CAREER BATTLES AND PATENT TROUBLES

Bell was making such good progress with the telephone that he hated to refocus on the harmonic telegraph. Time was growing shorter in the race to invent one, though, since the Pacific Telegraph Company had recently spent $750,000 to purchase a method of sending four messages at once. Bell knew that his competition was stiff. He worried about applying for the necessary patents before Elisha Gray's patents were processed.

Bell feared that his and Gray's processes of discovery would be close, and he worried that Gray's patents would be awarded over his. Heeding Hubbard's earlier advice to document his findings, even in letters, Bell wrote to his father about the patents and the multiple telegraph:

> In regard to the patents: My lawyers, Pollack and Baily, found on examination at the Patent Office, that I had developed the idea so much farther than Gray had done that they have applied for three distinct patents, in only one of which I

come into collision with Gray. The first patent covers the principle of "Multiple Telegraphy," basing my claim upon the instruments exhibited. (These instruments require *two* lines, an up-line and down-line.) The second patent covers the principle of using the *Induced Current*, so as to permit a single wire to be employed. The third patent is for a "vibratory Circuit breaker" for the purpose of converting the Vibratory motion of my Receiving Instrument into a permanent *make or break* of a local circuit.[42]

In the letter, Bell emphasized the three specific patents that he would use when working on the multiple telegraph and the processes involved, just in case he needed additional documentation later. Also in this letter, Bell explained to his father why his invention would be so beneficial and why Western Union was interested in it:

> Now my invention comes along as a means by which thirty or forty messages may be sent simultaneously, and by which intermediate stations may communicate with one another. . . . At all events it is evidently a good time to bring out the invention. I visited the Western Union telegraph headquarters in New York on my way here. I have made arrangements to spend Saturday and Sunday every week in New York at the West. Un. Building.[43]

Unfortunately, Bell's confidence in Western Union was soon shattered. When he gave a successful demonstration of his harmonic telegraph to Western Union, the company's officials claimed that they had Elisha Gray's experiments in their back room and did not need to purchase Bell's machine.

Bell was furious with Western Union and frustrated with the harmonic telegraph. He accused the officials of spying and stormed out of their offices. Exhausted, disappointed, and sick of the harmonic telegraph, he turned all of his attention and effort back to the telephone.

He explained in detail the process of the telephone to Hubbard, who finally showed a small interest in the invention. Again, Hubbard encouraged Bell to make a written record of his work. Hubbard then filed the patent documents, which explained the functions of the device.

HUBBARD'S CONCERNS ABOUT BELL

Backing Bell's experiments was one matter, but Hubbard believed that turning

FIRST SIGNS OF PATENT PROBLEMS

Bell stated in a letter to his father, dated February 1876—the same day he met with Zenas Frank Wilber, a patent attorney—that the conflicts with his patent and Gray's patent arose immediately. This letter is taken from the Alexander Graham Bell Family Papers *collection.*

"The Examiner was about to issue my Patent when he discovered that Mr. Gray had applied for a Caveat for something similar before my Patent appeared. . . . It was then my right to see the portions of Mr. Gray's specification which came into conflict with mine. . . . Mr. Gray made a sudden change in the intensity of the current without actually making or breaking the current. . . . I explained that. . . I had mentioned the same thing in my application filed February, 1875 just one year ago. The Examiner handed me my papers of the date and I was able to point out the exact passage describing what Mr. Gray has only now taken out a Caveat for. The Examiner said that was so and that he had not noticed that passage before as bearing on the subject. He allowed me to make an amendment . . . and the Patent was handed in this morning. . . . If I succeed in securing that patent without interference from the others—the whole thing is mine—and I am sure of fame, fortune and success if I can only persevere in perfecting my apparatus."

HUBBARD'S ULTIMATUM TO BELL

Mabel's father, Gardiner Greene Hubbard, told Bell to give up the telephone, and concentrate on the telegraph if he ever hoped to marry Mabel. In response, Bell wrote a huffy letter to Hubbard. His letter is part of the Alexander Graham Bell Family Papers *collection.*

"I shall certainly not relinquish my profession until I find something more profitable (which will be difficult), nor until I have qualified others to work in the same field. . . .

Should Mabel come to love me as devotedly as I love her—she will not object to any work in which I may be engaged as long as it is honorable and profitable. If she does not come to love me well enough to accept me whatever my profession or business may be—I do not want her at all! I do not want a half-love, nor do I want her to marry my profession."

over his daughter to the dreamer was another. At one point, Hubbard even threatened to forbid the two to marry if Bell did not cease work on the telephone until he had made the multiple telegraph a success. In a heated letter dated April 26, 1876, Hubbard told Bell,

If you could work as other men do you would accomplish much more than with your present habits. . . . While you are flying from one thing to another you may accidently accomplish something but you probably will never perfect anything. . . . If you could make one good invention in the telegraph field you would secure an annual income as much as a Professorship and then you could settle that on your wife and teach Visible Speech and experiment in telegraphy with an easy and undisturbed conscience.[44]

Although her father had concerns, Mabel did not. She had grown fonder of Bell as she spent more time with him, even though she was at first taken aback by the affection he gave her, especially after thinking of him only as a teacher. In time, however, she found herself admiring and respecting his passion and dedication to his work.

In the fall of 1865, and only a few months before his success with the telephone, Bell happily listened to Mabel officially welcome his love interest. At this time she was eighteen, slender, and had soft brown hair. Bell was twenty-eight, stood a head taller than Mabel, and had

Mabel and Alexander stand on Sable Island, looking toward the sea.

grown a thick dark beard. On Thanksgiving Day, while Mabel walked with Bell in the garden outside her parents' home, she accepted his marriage proposal. A letter she wrote to a friend described her feelings on their engagement:

> I told him I loved him better than anybody but Mamma and if he was satisfied with so much love I would be engaged to him that very day! . . . He almost refused to let me bind myself to him. He reminded me I had not seen other men. But I told him I could never find anyone to love as well, so he submitted very cheerfully to the engagement, only he wants me to understand that it is *I* who did it, and of course *he* could not refuse a lady![45]

It was not long before Mabel became Bell's greatest supporter, no matter what her father thought of Bell as a future son-in-law.

Bell understood Hubbard's perspective, but after his successful test with the telephone, he did not devote any more time to the multiple telegraph. Mabel's pride had also bolstered his determination, and he had no doubts that the telephone would become a bigger success than any multiple telegraph that Gray or Western Union could manufacture.

5 Introducing the Telephone to the World

As the summer of 1876 approached, Bell had two main priorities: First, he needed to give public demonstrations of the telephone, and second, he needed to increase his income. Giving the demonstrations worried him more than increasing his income.

Bell knew that he could always go back to teaching and tutoring to earn a regular wage, but traveling with the telephone to different cities was risky. It was not nearly as reliable as teaching. With his limited mechanical and electrical knowledge, Bell worried that problems such as broken

With inventors like Thomas Edison seeking to improve upon the telephone, Bell was constantly under pressure to perfect his invention.

Bell's pass to the International Centennial Exhibition in Philadelphia.

phone as perfect as possible. He had to do this before other inventors could come up with improvements and also file patents.

THE FIRST MAJOR DEMONSTRATION

During this period of his life, twenty-nine-year-old Bell had given up on the harmonic telegraph and had more time for other interests. He decided to resume teaching during the daytime so that he could earn a regular wage. During the evenings he worked on perfecting his inventions.

So far, Bell had demonstrated the telephone only to small groups in the Boston area. His main worry was the possibility of parts breaking during the travels to each new location. Bell knew that if he could not make the repairs on his own, then the telephone would not function. If that happened, Bell also knew that the telephone would not be considered a major invention.

He shared his concerns with Mabel about transporting the telephone too far. He also said that he did not want to neglect his students by spending too much time showing the telephone to buyers or investors.

parts could cause the demonstrations to fail.

Eventually, with Mabel's encouragement, Bell did begin demonstrating the telephone at many public events. When problems arose, he worked hard to solve them. Soon other inventors recognized the potential of his great invention and Bell faced competition to make his tele-

Mabel understood Bell's worries. Traveling was not always comfortable, nor was it easy to protect valuables during the shipping process. She also knew Bell well enough to realize that he was experiencing some anxiety about putting his reputation on the line with the telephone. As summer edged closer, Mabel believed that the greatest opportunity to demonstrate the telephone would be at the International Centennial Exhibition in Philadelphia. The exhibition would take place in June, and it was a huge industrial fair where many nations sent their leaders to learn about the latest inventions in technology. The inventors who won awards for their exhibits also received a lot of publicity from newspapers, and this is what Mabel hoped would happen to Bell.

Convincing Bell that he should send his telephone to the exhibition would not be easy, though. His anxiety increased when he realized that Elisha Gray's inventions would be in a large, fancy Western Union exhibit. Bell worried that his telephone would not be noticed without a big company backing his display. Every time Mabel mentioned the exhibition, Bell would offer reasons why he did not have time to enter the telephone as an electrical exhibit.

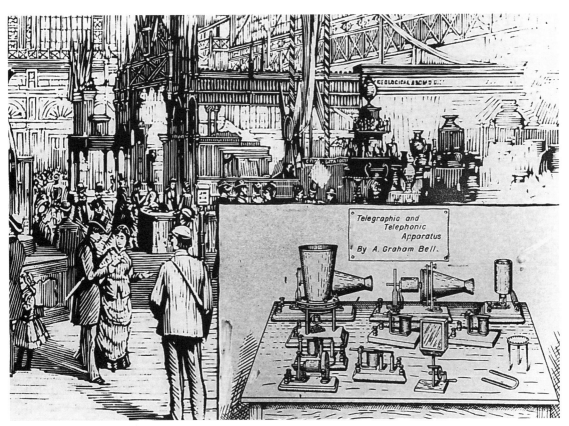

The hall where Bell displayed his telephone at the 1876 Centennial Exhibition in Philadelphia.

First, he made excuses about the machine not being perfect enough to demonstrate at such a major event. When that reason did not change Mabel's mind, he claimed that his students needed help studying for their examinations. His stalling caused him to miss the deadline to enter his invention in the electrical division of the exhibition.

Even this setback did not stop Mabel. She chose not to give up and convinced Bell that his telephone could be entered in the educational division. Her strategy worked, and he decided to enter the telephone in the exhibition along with his other teaching devices, such as the glove with letters and a visible speech chart. He still refused to go to Philadelphia to demonstrate the telephone himself, however.

Mabel knew that Bell needed to show off his invention in person if he hoped for it to stand out amidst the other exhibits. She strongly believed that showcasing the telephone at this particular event would be important to their future. Risking Bell's anger, she came up with a plan that tricked him into going.

A few days after Bell had sent his inventions to Philadelphia, Mabel arrived at the Boston School for the Deaf just as he dismissed his classes one afternoon. She met him at the school in a carriage, and offered to take him for a ride to help him relax. It was a hot afternoon, and Bell hated the heat. He happily climbed aboard the carriage and settled in next to his future wife. One biographer describes how easily Mabel had Bell under her spell:

After nearly a week of being on the defensive with everyone, Alec [she had asked him to drop the k] found her gentle, innocent and loving presence very soothing. He climbed in beside her and really relaxed as they drove down the lovely, tree-shaded Cambridge streets. . . . It wasn't until the carriage drew in close to the Cambridge railroad station that poor Alec woke to the fact that once again his Mabel was winding him around her little finger.[46]

Sitting in front of the train station, Bell argued with Mabel. His faced reddened as he reminded her that he did not have a ticket to Philadelphia. Mabel reached into her purse and pulled out a ticket. He complained that he did not have a suitcase, but then the carriage driver raised a packed bag over the seat and handed it to him. When he realized that he was out of honest excuses, he shouted at her, saying he was not going under any circumstances. Mabel burst into tears and threatened not to marry him if he did not do this since it could help secure their financial future.

Although Bell was furious because of the time and money that would be wasted traveling and spending a week in another town, he boarded the hot train to Philadelphia. After he arrived, he soon discovered more severe problems than just lost time or money. Just as he had always feared, his telephone apparatus had been damaged in shipping, and Bell had to do some quick repairs to have it in good shape for the judges. To make mat-

MABEL'S INFLUENCE ON BELL'S SUCCESS

When Mabel Hubbard prompted her future husband to demonstrate the telephone, she acted on a deep belief in his abilities. In Helen Waite's Make a Joyful Sound, *these emotions are made clear in a letter that Mabel wrote after Bell left for Philadelphia in June 1876.*

"How shall I tell you enough how happy and glad I am that you are in Philadelphia with all the distinguished scientists who will understand and appreciate you and your discoveries. I have been so unhappy and worried about the thing for so long, I can hardly breathe freely yet, but the more I think about it the more relieved I am.

It was very hard to send you off so unwillingly but I was sure it was for the best and you would be glad of it by and by. Mamma had a long letter from Papa telling her his reasons for wanting you. I am so very glad you have gone for I know you will succeed. . . .

Don't get discouraged now, if you but persevere success must come. Anyway, it will be a great help to you to be connected with scientific men. I've been thinking about you every spare moment. . . . How I miss you. . . . With a heartful of love to you dear,
Lovingly, Mabel."

ters worse, Bell needed to find another person to help him demonstrate the telephone, but that dilemma was solved when Mabel's cousin agreed to help him.

Bell also learned that Western Union had indeed bought the rights to Elisha Gray's latest inventions, which would be judged the same day as Bell's telephone. And just as Bell thought, Gray's versions of the multiple telegraph and a harmonic telegraph were on display in the posh Western Union exhibit. A letter written to his parents on June 25, 1876, clearly shows Bell's worry regarding Gray and Western Union:

I am afraid also that the effects I can produce will be much feebler than his as he has every advantage that the Western Union Telegraph Company can give him. My only chance consists in having my apparatus for the transmission of vocal sounds a success. If I am allowed to talk and explain I am alright—for I am sure of my theory.[47]

Bell's admission that a verbal demonstration was necessary to impress the judges is ironic considering that he never wanted to be in Philadelphia in the first place. And although Bell believed

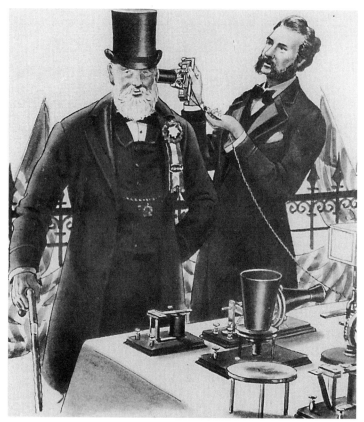

Bell demonstrates the telephone for Dom Pedro, emperor of Brazil and one of the international leaders at the 1876 Centennial Exhibition.

to the exhibits that sweltering day were two prominent men: Sir William Thompson, a famous English scientist, and Dom Pedro II, the emperor of Brazil. Dom Pedro had visited Bell several days earlier at the Boston School for the Deaf during the emperor's tour of successful American schools for the deaf.

The judges drifted through the long hall, edging closer to Bell, but by this time of the day they were growing hot, exhausted, and irritable. They discussed their uncomfortable circumstances and decided not to judge any more exhibits that day. Then Dom Pedro saw Bell across the room, and he called out to the familiar face.

The Brazilian emperor was a short, energetic, portly man. When he headed for Bell's table, the others followed. In an article later written by Fred De Land for *Popular Science,* he described how Dom Pedro swayed the judges to take a closer look at Bell's inventions: "His Majesty spoke so enthusiastically about the telephone, that, tired as the judges were, they concluded to investigate thoroughly its merits."[48]

Thompson took an immediate interest in the apparatus. When the notable English scientist put the receiving end to his ear, Bell went to the other side of his exhibit area with one of the sending

completely in his telephone, his earlier concern that the Western Union exhibit would draw more attention was well founded. His invention was nearly hidden in a far corner of the exhibit hall. Bell knew it would take a great deal of luck for the judges to even notice his inventions in that location. They could easily walk right down the middle of the hall and never give him or the telephone a second glance.

JUDGED BY HIS PEERS

Despite all of the problems, luck was on Bell's side. Walking along with the judges transmitters. As Bell spoke and sang into the transmitter, Thompson ran back to Bell to tell him that he had heard him clearly.

Dom Pedro did not want to miss out on this miracle, so this time he took the receiver. His excitement upon hearing Bell recite Shakespeare could not be contained. He jumped out of his chair, yelling, "I have heard, I have heard."[49]

Dom Pedro's presence, and his enthusiasm, that sultry day in Philadelphia was an unexpected bit of luck for Bell and a real boost for the overall success of the telephone.

THE FIRST PUBLIC RESPONSE

The judges were amazed by Bell's invention. One of the experts, Professor George F. Barker of the University of Pennsylvania, had this to say about the simple yet ingenious device:

> I was greatly astonished and delighted to hear *for the first time* the transmission of articulate speech electrically. The mode of operation of the instrument was obvious at once, as soon as it was exhibited: it was one of those marvelously simple inventions that causes one to wonder, on seeing it for the first time, that it had not been invented long before.[50]

Although Barker's words certainly revealed his excitement for the telephone, Joseph Henry of the Smithsonian Institution summed up the unanimous feeling of the judges that day. In his "General Report of the Judges," Henry stated that the tele-

phone was "the greatest marvel hitherto achieved by the telegraph."[51]

All of the people who witnessed Bell's telephone at the International Centennial Exhibition realized that the device had the potential to change their lives. Bell knew, however, that he still had important groundwork to lay before the telephone could become widely used.

So far, the device had only been tested across short distances. Bell needed to ensure that the telephone would work over great distances and carry multiple signals.

MORE EXPERIMENTS

Bell received a Certificate of Award and a medal for his invention. After the judging on June 25, Bell headed back to Boston to help his students with their final exams. As soon as the tests were completed, he and Thomas Watson gathered the necessary materials for their continued experiments and departed for Brantford.

As was his custom over the past few years, Bell frequently returned to his parents' home in Brantford during the summer months. Watson accompanied him this trip to continue their improvements on the telephone. The two men worked furiously, stringing stovepipe wire from Bell's parents' house to the telegraph line at Mount Pleasant, Ontario, located a few miles away.

When the job of laying the wire was completed, Bell and Watson then installed a sending device at Brantford and a receiving device at Mount Pleasant. Everything worked well with the initial trial, so the men began moving the wires greater distances apart to test how far telephone communication could be transmitted.

These experiments, along with the constant task of laying wire, had the Brantford neighbors talking about the men. Some thought that they were a little crazy; others thought that Bell and Watson might be brilliant scientists. At the very least, most people considered them an interesting pair to watch that summer. One neighbor, William Brooks, remembered the day that Bell came across his father's property asking if he could string the wire straight along their fence line:

Well along came our neighbor, young Mr. Bell, carrying a coil of wire. He said there was to be a test of the telephone that evening and he wanted to run a line out to the Mount Pleasant Road. Could he string it along our fences. That was quite a problem. It was his idea to string the wire right across our gateway, which would make it impossible to get in or out with our loads.[52]

The neighbor was friendly and wanted to help Bell but explained that he needed to have the gateway open until he har-

An engraving of an early switchboard.

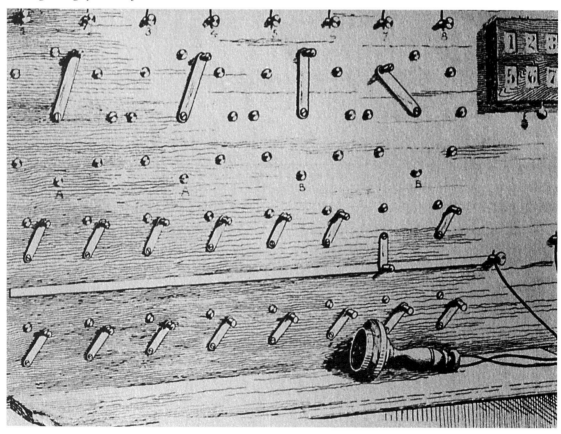

BELL'S ANXIETY ABOUT GRAY AT THE EXHIBITION

After Bell learned that Sir William Thompson and Dom Pedro wanted to view Elisha Gray's device at the same time that they viewed Bell's, he wrote a letter to Mabel about his fears. Bell's letter is included in the Alexander Graham Bell Family Papers.

"He [Thompson] stated that he was coming to the Building on Sunday with the Emperor Dom Pedro—see Mr. Gray's instruments and asked me to exhibit mine at the same time!

I must say I don't like this at all—and would rather avoid a direct collision with Mr. Gray if possible.

However, I suppose fate has decided! And it must be done. I feel very nervous about it—for I feel I have come on here very hurriedly without sufficient preparation to be thrown into direct collision with Mr. Gray.

Mr. Gray has command of a large battery power—and had every facility for a successful experiment—whereas I have few facilities—and I have no one to help me. . . .

I can talk and explain and Sir William will understand. I can at all events show him I have the theory even if my exhibit will not stand a show beside Gray's. . . .

Let us hope for the best—but I must say that your poor Alec feels very hopeless and heartbroken about it."

vested his crop for the day. He did offer to help Bell string the wire after he had finished his own work.

One major breakthrough during these experiments came when Bell used already existing telegraph lines to transmit three singers' voices in Brantford to Paris, Ontario, approximately eight miles away. He hooked up a three-way mouthpiece and the singers' distinct voices could be heard. The distance of this test was only one of the important aspects. The three-way mouthpiece also proved that multiple signals could be transmitted over one line.

TROUBLE WITH WESTERN UNION

Not everyone was pleased with Bell's success. Elisha Gray had listened through the receiver that June afternoon at the exhibition and wondered if Bell's telephone was really anything more than an acoustic trick. Some historians believe that Gray had experimented with similar devices but could not make them function; therefore, he doubted Bell's working design.

Many of these experts also feel that Gray's motives to discredit Bell were related to the enormous impact of such an invention. The telephone promised to change the way the world communicated from 1876 onward, and some historians believe that Gray wanted to be a part of those advances.

Even with these amazing leaps of progress, Bell was still financially frustrated. He needed money to marry Mabel, and he believed that the most logical solution to his money problems would be to sell his rights to the telephone. Because of Gardiner Greene Hubbard's patent experience, Bell discussed his idea with his future father-in-law.

Both Bell and Hubbard knew that the head of Western Union, William Orton, who had at first dismissed the telephone as a passing toy, was now interested in the device. Bell also believed that Western Union's well-built telegraph lines would decrease the static that sometimes occurred on the smaller lines that he used during his experiments.

Even though Hubbard and Orton had argued in the past, especially about the multiple telegraph that Bell had shown to Western Union, Hubbard agreed to approach Orton. Biographer Edwin S. Grosvenor describes the meeting between these two powerful and competing businessmen:

BELL'S DESIRE TO MARRY AND SETTLE DOWN

Even with the early success and responsibilities of the telephone occupying his time, Bell still ached to make Mabel Hubbard his wife. In a letter dated April 9, 1877, included in the Alexander Graham Bell Family Papers, *he poured out his dreams of making a home with her.*

"My dear loving little girl,

What little bird whispers into your ears—the time to write and what to say? What good angel dictates your loving words to me? Your perfect love and trust Mabel are a delight and I feel quite selfish to remain unsatisfied. But patience is difficult when home is so far away. . . . I often feel as if I shall go mad with the feverish anxiety of my unsettled life. Thank heaven you do know not what it is to be drifting about the world by yourself—without a place you can call your own—and hardly a friend that is more than a passing acquaintance.

I do so long to have a house of my own—with you to share it—and the older I grow the more feverishly impatient am I to obtain it.

I have grown mercenary and selfish about it—and I am beginning to look at everything from the dollar and cents point of view."

Late in 1876, when Gardiner Hubbard offered to sell Western Union the rights to the Bell telephone for $100,000, Orton turned it down, apparently still smarting from his old rivalry . . . and so the most rational course for everyone—to incorporate Bell telephones into Western Union's impressive existing wire network was lost. William Orton became the man who refused to buy the most profitable invention in recorded history.[53]

Orton refused to buy the rights to the telephone because he had enlisted other inventors to try to copy Bell's invention. Among those inventors were Elisha Gray and Thomas Edison.

Bell was greatly worried to have these inventive minds working on a competing apparatus for Western Union. He was also disheartened because, without the money from selling the rights, he could not yet marry Mabel. In addition, Bell needed to raise funds to file patents for the telephone in Europe. Doing this would give him exclusive right to the telephone overseas as well as in the United States.

Now, not only would he have to postpone marriage because he lacked enough money, but he would also have to spend what money he did have to start his own company. The only good thing that Bell had going for him at this time was the fact Hubbard agreed to guide him as he started the telephone business.

BELL TELEPHONE COMPANY

Hubbard was a shrewd businessman, however, and the inventor and his partners decided to lease the telephones rather than to sell them to customers. This would bring money into the company each month instead of on a one-time sale.

In July 1877, one of their first customers requested a line from his shop in Boston to his home. The customer was Bell's old acquaintance Charles Williams, whom Watson had worked for when he met Bell.

With the improvements that had been made to the telephone, Bell was not as worried about showing his invention to the public. He began giving demonstrations throughout the fall of 1876 and into the early part of 1877. With each event more people fell in love with Bell telephones, and they began ordering them for their own use. During this time of demonstrating the telephone, Bell became known for using the expression "Hoy, Hoy" as his first greeting.

Over time, the same confidence and ability that he exhibited while teaching came through in his demonstrations. His commanding, theatrical presence—inherited from his grandfather—and his good-natured personality—inherited from his father—intrigued the crowds. Bell finally learned to have fun with the people who attended the lectures, even though they rarely made him any money. For example, one biographer gave this description of a public demonstration in Salem, Massachusetts, on February 12, 1877:

> He spoke over an eighteen-mile telephone connection to Watson in their

The Telephone.

FOR CHEAP AND QUICK COMMUNICATION, BY DIRECT SPEECH.

TIME AND DISTANCE OVERCOME.

THE SPEAKING TELEPHONE of PROF. ALEXANDER GRAHAM BELL has now attained to such simplicity and cheapness, as render it universally available for public, private, social or business communications.

Using no battery (unless a loud call-bell is required), and no moving machinery, the Telephone is perfectly clean, and always ready, in any office or household where instantaneous communication with any other point is desired. It needs only a wire between the two stations, and NO SKILL is required by the users, except to speak plainly and listen attentively. The instrument is neat and portable, and an ornament to any room or office.

The Telephone conveys the *quality* of the voice, so that the person speaking can be recognised at the other end of the line. It transmits names, figures, foreign words, or plain English, with equal facility, and as fast as the person speaking would ordinarily converse with one in the same room. It enables the manufacturer to talk with his factory superintendent, the main office with the branch office, the house with the store, the country residence with the stables or any part of the grounds, the mouth of the mine with its remotest workings, or, in short, any given point with any other point, although many miles apart.

The YEARLY cost to the lessee for a set of Telephones—one at each end of his line—is TWENTY DOLLARS. The Proprietors keep the instruments in repair, without charge, and the lessee has NO EXPENSE in working them.

Patent rights have been granted for the Telephone, in Canada, the United States, and foreign countries.

Information will be given, Telephones leased, or local Agents appointed for any part of the Dominion of Canada, on application to

THOMAS HENDERSON.

An early Canadian advertisement for Bell's telephone details its potential uses to prospective buyers.

laboratory in Boston. Watson could be heard by those in the hall, shouting, "Hoy! Hoy!" Bell happily transmitted to Boston the news story dictated by a reporter for the Boston *Globe*. Next day, the paper published it, under the trumpeting headline: "SENT BY TELEPHONE. The First Newspaper Dispatch Sent by a Human Voice Over the Wires."[54]

Bell, however, was not the only person earning praise and applause for demonstrating a working telephone device. Throughout the spring of 1877, Elisha Gray had been showing a telephone apparatus that he and the other Western Union inventors had built. In this model, Edison had come up with a compressed piece of carbon that was secured to a metal diaphragm that took the place of the stretched rubber membrane.

This slight alteration in the telephone's construction made a great improvement in the volume and clarity of speakers' voices. It gave the necessary vibration, but it did not vibrate so much that it caused distortion of voices, which sometimes occurred with the stretched membranes.

When stories that Gray had invented the telephone started appearing in newspapers, Bell was hurt. He could not understand why anyone would print such lies about him. He immediately sent letters of complaint, confronting the published claims that Gray had invented the telephone. In one such letter, dated March 2, 1877, Bell emphasized to Gray that his definition of a telephone is for an apparatus that transmits the voice, and he had no knowledge of Gray's ever inventing such a device.

Bell received an apologetic reply from Gray that would prove to be a valuable document in a future lawsuit. In the letter, Gray stated,

> I do not however claim even the credit of inventing it, as I do not believe a mere description of an idea that has never been reduced to practice—in the strict sense of that phrase—should be dignified with the name invention.[55]

Bell accepted the letter as Gray's word that Bell indeed had the right to claim the telephone as his invention. With the arrival of the letter, as well as a great increase in orders for Bell telephones, the inventor was finally able to focus on marriage. Even Mabel's parents realized the need for Bell to slow down. They encouraged Bell and Mabel to wed, which made Bell so ecstatic that he immediately wrote to his parents, "In fact they urge me very strongly to marry at once. . . . They say that I will never be well and strong until I have some one to look after me."[56]

In a quiet ceremony in her parents' home on July 11, 1877, Mabel Hubbard married Alexander Graham Bell. As a wedding present, Bell gave Mabel a cross made out of eleven little pearls. He also gave his bride 1,497 shares of his stock in the Bell Telephone Company, keeping only ten shares for himself. This generous monetary gift ensured Mabel of the financial security that worried her enough to trick him into boarding that train to Philadelphia.

The newlyweds journeyed to Brantford, Ontario, so that Mabel could meet her husband's family. Then the young couple set off for England, where they hoped to enjoy a long honeymoon and market the telephone. Bell knew that further demonstrations were needed in England to guarantee the continued success of the first telephone company and to secure his English patent.

Chapter

6 Mass Communication and Controversy

As Bell traveled with Mabel aboard the SS *Anchoria* to Europe, he reviewed his plans to make England the starting point for establishing the telephone worldwide. At the time, he did not realize just how much the telephone would extend communication or how much controversy it would cause.

The Bells were completely surprised and disheartened by the controversy that soon emerged over the rights to the telephone. The popularity of the telephone and the arguments buzzing about who really invented it, thrust Alexander Graham Bell into the public spotlight. He became one of the most recognizable names in newspapers around the world in the next year.

SETTLING INTO ENGLAND

When the young couple reached England, they were welcomed by Sir William Thompson, the English scientist who had first tested Bell's telephone at the International Centennial Exhibition and had since become a major supporter of the invention. Thompson helped Bell arrange to demonstrate the device for important people.

Although Mabel knew that her husband had planned to combine some business with their honeymoon, she soon realized that the trip had turned into a revolving episode of scientific discussions centered around the telephone. It was also obvious that the excursion would last much longer than they had first planned. Bell chose to stay in England until the next summer so that he could discuss and demonstrate the telephone to potential customers.

Mabel was a little disappointed at first, but she knew that Bell needed to demonstrate the telephone in England. He also needed to file the patents for the invention while they were there and possibly set up an English branch of the Bell Telephone Company.

Another reason why the Bells decided to extend their stay in England was because Mabel was expecting their first child, and her doctor had advised her against embarking on the long voyage home. While settling in for the extended stay, Mabel fell in love with the spacious Kensington house in which they lived. Bell turned his attention toward converting two of the large rooms into working

An engraving of Bell demonstrating his telephone.

laboratories for his continuous experiments. They also spent a great deal of time entertaining Bell's scientific and business friends in their home.

Bell continued his lectures and demonstrations, and Mabel worked as his secretary, taking dictation by reading his lips and then writing letters. Because she could read German, she also translated German scientific papers and books for Bell, either by reading them aloud to him or writing down the important aspects he needed for his research.

THE QUEEN'S APPROVAL

On January 14, 1878, as Bell tinkered with ways to improve the quality of the telephone's sound and its ability to transmit over longer distances, he received an invitation to present his telephone to Queen Victoria. Bell knew that the queen's approval of the telephone would help establish its credibility as an asset to the communication system in England. He looked forward to the possible positive impact that this important demonstration would hold for the telephone's future.

On the day of the demonstration, the queen listened with interest as Bell explained his invention. Bell then told her that he had previously arranged for people in three different English cities to send messages through the telephone that evening. There were singers in Cowes, a bugler in Southampton, and an organist in London.

When Bell handed Queen Victoria the receiver, the performers took turns sending their messages on the telephone and the queen listened, first in astonishment and then with delight.

Her reaction caused a murmur among the crowd that was present, and the Queen's attention was diverted temporarily from the telephone. As one of the singers began again, Bell softly touched the queen's hand to encourage her to listen. Touching the queen in any form broke all rules of the royal court and a gasp arose from the people near enough to see the gesture.

To Bell, who lived with and taught people with hearing difficulties, the gentle gesture was quite natural. In English society, however, any informal touching of royalty was considered extremely impolite. Queen Victoria did not seem at all bothered by the gesture, though, and when Bell motioned for her to listen to the receiver, she once again showed great interest.

MABEL'S FEELINGS ABOUT STAYING IN ENGLAND

In a letter included in Helen Waite's Make a Joyful Noise *Mabel wrote to her mother, sending the news of their plans to stay on in England.*

"I have not written before, because I dreaded telling you of our plans. . . . Alec has decided to remain here until next summer. He says that in America there are plenty of men who know all about the telephone and its management, but here there is no-one but himself. Then there are the foreign patents. And some gentlemen here have agreed to organize a company to control the patents here, and they say they must have Alec's presence for at least the first year. He thinks he is more sure of a good income here than at home."

Queen Victoria's approval of the telephone was important to Bell, who thought it would establish his credibility in Europe, help his sales, and secure him patent rights.

Queen Victoria was so impressed that two days later she asked to purchase the telephones Bell that had shown her. Although he could not sell the only two that he had with him, he felt confident that her approval would help establish a telephone system in England.

ESTABLISHING THE TELEPHONE IN ENGLAND

Even with Queen Victoria's approval of the telephone, Bell ran into a stumbling block when seeking an English patent for the telephone. Similar to the events in the

United States with Elisha Gray and Western Union, rival telephone companies in England claimed that Bell had no right to an English patent. As Bell explained to Mabel, the problem stemmed from a previously published paper about the telephone: "You see, May [his name for her], under English law, if an invention is published before patent is taken out, the inventor loses his rights to it."[57]

Their friend Sir William Thompson, who had been so enthusiastic about Bell's invention, had inadvertently caused the problem. He had spoken to various groups in England about the telephone and also had a paper published in the British scientific magazine *Nature*. Thompson felt bad about the well-intentioned mistake, and he stood before the patent court, announcing that he had lectured about the telephone on Bell's behalf. Without much more controversy, the judge and jury decreed that Alexander Graham Bell indeed had the right to his English patent.

After winning the patent, Bell tried to convince England's major businesses of the practicalities of the telephone. On March 25, 1878, he sent a letter to a group of investors that stated why the telephone would make a worthy investment for them:

> The great advantage it possesses over every other form of electrical apparatus consists in the fact that it requires no skill to operate the instrument. All other telegraph machines produce signals which require to be translated by experts, and such instruments are therefore extremely limited in their application, but the telephone actually speaks, and for this reason it can be utilized for nearly every purpose for which speed is employed.[58]

Also in the spring of 1878, Bell sent a letter to the Electric Speaking Telephone Company outlining his ideas for the telephone's ability to increase immediate communication. He suggested that the devices could be rented to public facilities, such as hospitals, railway stations, and even hotels, using a system similar to the telegraph wires. Bell even suggested that the cables eventually could be laid underground for better durability and less damage from weather. If cities used his ideas for the cable system, Bell believed that many cities could be connected to each other. And when more cable was laid, then countries could be connected to each other. Eventually, using these cables—much like the telegraph cables—people could communicate with each other immediately. The difference would be that people would communicate in their own home or business instead of relying on a telegraph message to be interpreted at a telegraph office and then forwarded to them by a messenger.

England was not open to Bell's visions for the telephone, however, and the investors chose not to put their money behind his invention. Also, the companies that Bell had hoped would lease the telephones did not share his vision. In spite of the impressive demonstrations, the companies were apprehensive and did not see much use for the telephone beyond the short distance communication they had witnessed with their own eyes.

One bright spot during this disappointing period came on May 8, 1878, with the birth of the Bells' daughter, Elsie May. Their joy did not last long, however, because back in the United States the war between Western Union and the Bell Telephone Company continued to rage.

MORE PATENT PROBLEMS AND LAWSUITS

Bell Telephone Company had been in stiff competition with its major rival, Western Union, which was still headed by William Orton. During December 1877 Orton had been confident that Hubbard, even with the success of Bell's telephone, could not afford to challenge him and the Western Union monopoly. Orton, therefore, had begun his own telephone

The main convenience of the telephone was that it allowed people to talk to one another from their homes, thus avoiding the lines and translators at a telegraph office.

Bell Telephone Company employees erect new poles and string wire.

company called the American Speaking Telephone Company.

Although Bell had written and filed patents for each step of the telephone's inventive process, including updates and innovations, Orton ignored the legality of the Bell Telephone Company's claims. Orton continued to make statements to newspapers claiming that Bell was not the true inventor of the telephone.

To make matters worse, the telephone lines that Western Union used were adapted into its already working system of telegraph wires. This gave Western Union a big advantage over the Bell Telephone Company during 1877 and 1878. Bell Telephone had to erect new poles and string new wires to reach communities that did not have telephone service. Not only did this process take a great deal of time, but it also sapped the company's finances.

Hubbard knew something drastic needed to be done to save the Bell Telephone Company from bankruptcy. He decided to sue Western Union for claiming that Alexander Graham Bell was not the true inventor of the telephone. Hubbard also hired Theodore Vail, a former employee of the U.S. Postal Service's railway mail service, as general manager of the company. Vail's enthusiasm to fight for the Bell Telephone Company was exactly what Hubbard needed. One biographer describes Vail's aggressive stance: "Vail's first act was to send a copy of the Bell patent to all Bell agents and advise them to stand firm against Western Union harassment and infringement."[59]

The company also needed more investors to purchase stock in Bell Telephone. Because of Western Union's

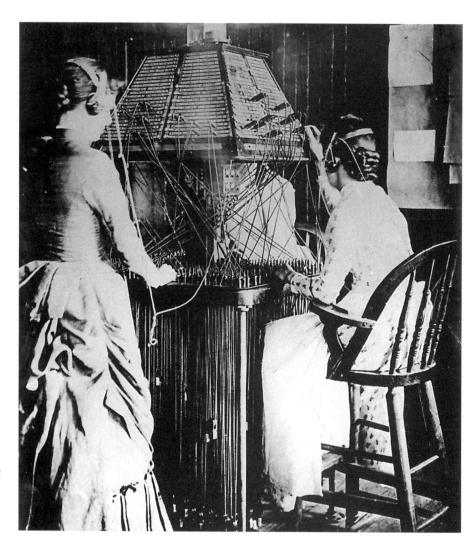

Women operate a switchboard in Richmond, Virginia.

success, investors had not been buying any more Bell Telephone stock. In January 1879 Hubbard found an ally in wealthy investor William H. Forbes. Forbes, along with other Boston financiers, took a chance on investing in Bell Telephone. With their additional money and Vail's management, Bell Telephone battled along in Western Union's shadow.

As the telephone companies fought to win customers, Americans slowly warmed to the idea of the telephone. They also learned skills that would place them in jobs for the telephone companies. Towns such as Seattle, that had economies based on wood products, saw a big increase in their income as they manufactured the tall poles needed for stringing telephone wires.

The telephone companies also offered more employment opportunities for women than any other companies had previously allowed. A great number of women went to work as telephone operators as well as cable testers in factories. A career as an operator was soon listed as one of the highest employment possibilities for women—second only to teaching. In rural areas of the western states, some women were even allowed to climb the tall poles and install telephone lines.

As the telephone's impact spread throughout the country, both as a communication tool and as a stronghold for the economies of many cities, Hubbard knew that he and Bell had to win the patent fight.

BELL WOULD BE THE KEY TO VICTORY

Hubbard cabled Bell in England, asking him to send any letters and newspaper clippings that might help document his claim to the telephone. Bell was not happy about Hubbard's decision to sue Western Union. He hated the idea of fighting in court for what he knew was rightfully his. At the time he was so disgusted with Elisha Gray and Western Union that he wanted to turn his back on the telephone altogether. He told Hubbard that he planned to take his family to Canada and find a teaching job.

Knowing that the Bells were on their way from England to Canada, Hubbard persuaded Thomas Watson to help convince Bell to fight the court case, telling him,

> Unless you act quickly and get Mr. Bell back to Boston immediately, he will be too late to save the situation, and he will lose all rights! I think the only sure way to get Alec Bell here is for one of us to fetch him, and I believe you, Mr. Watson, are the right man to do it![60]

Watson decided to meet Bell and Mabel on the docks in Quebec, but first he stopped by his partner's old laboratory workshop. Knowing that his friend rarely cleaned the shop, Watson took a chance and found the letter from Elisha Gray in a trash can. With this evidence in hand, now all he had to do was convince Bell how important his actual presence was in court.

After welcoming the Bells back and helping them settle into Melville and Eliza Bell's Brantford home, Watson

Bell's Position with the Bell Telephone Company

In a letter dated March 1879, which is now part of the Alexander Graham Bell Family Papers, *Bell formally accepted a position proposed by then company president William H. Forbes and outlines his terms and required changes to the initial proposition.*

"My dear Sir:

Your favour of the 24th inst. was duly received. I am willing to conclude an agreement with the Company upon substantially the basis proposed in your letter. Your proposition—as I understand it—is as follows:

My salary is to be as before.

I am to give such time to legal suits as counsel may require.

I am to offer to the Company all results of my work— my experiments not being limited to telephone apparatus.

The Company is to pay me the cost of all experiments or work, the results of which it accepts.—In regard to these points, I should like to make a few remarks and suggestions—

My salary has not been $3000 per annum as you have supposed—but $5000— . . . I find it almost impossible to carry on Telephonic experiments without the aid of an assistant and I would recommend that the Company should pay his salary. . . .

It should be the understanding of both the parties to our agreement that no arrangement shall be made during its continuance with other parties which shall compromise my reputation as the original inventor of the Speaking Telephone, and that if any arrangement is made with other parties, I reserve to myself the right to terminate this agreement."

updated Bell on the court case. He also discussed the latest developments in the telephone's construction. Watson had developed a device to let the recipient of a telephone transmission know when the message was coming in. He told Bell how he had been working on a system that rang a bell when a transmission was being sent. The bell idea came to him because of the inventor's last name.

Even with Watson's strong persuasive abilities, Bell still resisted going to

Boston. At one exasperated moment, he even lashed out at his friend, saying,

> I want to make it very clear to you that I have grown very dissatisfied with the entire telephone business, Mr. Watson. I am not having anything more to do with it. I intend to devote my life to teaching. Will you please understand and believe I am serious about this?[61]

But Watson did not give up. He knew that Bell had a rightful claim to the invention and that their entire financial future rested on his willingness to fight for his invention. Finally, after many discussions, Watson convinced Bell that it was dishonorable to turn his back on his company's investors and employees. With that admonishment, Bell realized he had not been thinking about the bigger picture and everyone who would be affected by his decision. He agreed to appear in court.

THE VICTORY

On April 4, 1879, after the pretrial statements were taken and the trial had begun, Bell wrote to his father. He relayed his confidence in their case and thought that they had a good chance of winning the lawsuit: "First day of Elisha Gray's Cross-Examination just concluded. Everything coming out in our favour. Counsel hope to obtain injunction inside of three weeks."[62]

As the court case continued, Bell's testimony proved to be a most important fac-tor. With his charm and elegant speaking voice, he relayed his earliest ideas about the telephone as well as the process of its invention. He told the court all about the telephone's various modifications and produced notes and letters proving his claim to the patent.

The patents filed by Western Union inventors showed markedly different processes of invention. It was clear that

New innovations, such as a bell to signal incoming calls and a separate transmitter and receiver, made telephones more efficient and easier to use.

none of the inventors had stolen information from one another. A final blow to Western Union's defense was the letter that Gray had sent to Bell in 1877 stating that he had no claim to inventing the telephone. Following the presentation of that letter, Gray gave his spoken testimony in which he vowed that the letter was genuine. To Western Union's dismay, he further damaged their case by adding these words about the letter: "I must swear to it. You can swear at it."[63]

The lawyers for Western Union had heard enough and encouraged the giant company to settle the claim before the case went any farther. On November 10, 1879, Western Union signed a settlement agreement that gave all telephones, lines, switchboards, patent rights in telephony, and any pending claims belonging to Western Union to the Bell Telephone Company. This transfer had to occur with no profit to Western Union.

In turn, Bell Telephone agreed not to market any telegraph capabilities and to pay Western Union 20 percent of its income for the next seventeen years. With this major hurdle behind them, Bell and Hubbard watched their stock prices soar. They immediately welcomed the onslaught of investors who wanted to secure a financial handle on the telephone business.

A HUSBAND'S ADVICE TO HIS YOUNG WIFE

After returning from England, Bell left Mabel and Elsie with his parents in Brantford while he went to fight for the Bell Telephone Company. Later he wrote a letter to Mabel, offering ideas for clothing as well as behavior. His letter is included in the Alexander Graham Bell Family Papers.

"You would be careful to put on your dressing gown and stockings and slippers at night when you take Elsie—you are careful of everyone's health instead of your own. If you promise to take good care of yourself and not worry—your poor husband will do anything his little wife wants him to! There now—good night my own sweet darling—Kiss Elsie for me and my father and mother and cousins.

Try dear to know them all—perhaps my absence will tend to bring you all together. My father and mother love you very much and I want them to find out what a noble little wife I have got.

Try also to ingratiate yourself with your servants—try to think of their wants and do little things for their comfort—so as to force them to become attached to you.

Your loving husband,
Alec"

Even though the Bell Telephone Company would be challenged again in court over patent lawsuits, it never lost. The stress involved in the battles, however, did take their toll on Bell's health. He gained more weight than was healthy for his body size, and his hair began turning gray. His sleeping patterns became irregular, and many nights he never slept at all. The time that he could spend with Mabel became limited as he spent more hours tracking his written records of invention and giving court statements. For the sake of his health, he was thankful that the battle with Western Union was over.

Still, in the span of only three years, Bell had endured the greatest patent controversy in history and forever changed the world of mass communication with his telephone. This victory allowed Bell to finally turn his attention to something new.

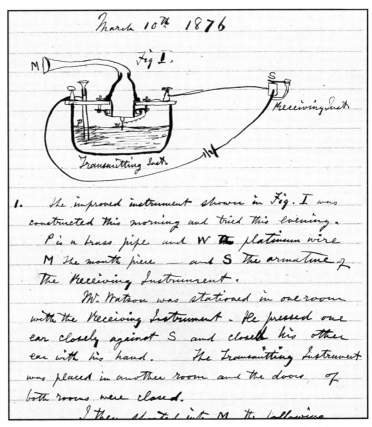

Bell's careful records and early telephone designs established him as the undisputed inventor of the telephone.

ANOTHER "PHONE"

When the telephone had become a dependable, readily available device in many homes, Bell worked on yet another idea he had for transmitting speech. Charles Sumner Tainter, an inventor whose work included the use of optical instruments, helped Bell with this device. Bell had been researching how optical instruments used light to receive and send airwaves, and he wanted to know if speech could be transmitted by light, too.

This time Bell did not plan on using any wires to send the connection electrically. Instead, Bell tried using selenium, a gray crystalline element, as an electrical connection. Selenium's electrical resistance varied under the action of light, and Bell was curious to see whether this element could replace the wires needed to make the telephone work.

By February 1880 Bell and Tainter had successfully transmitted speech over a beam of light with a device that Bell termed the *photophone*. In an article he wrote for *Popular Science,* Bell expressed his elation over the sounds that he had heard with this new invention. He also shared his thoughts on the photophone's impact in the realm of science:

> I have heard articulate speech produced by sunlight! I have heard a ray of the sun laugh and cough and sing . . . . In general science, discoveries will be made by the Photophone that are undreamed of just now.[64]

Bell's excitement about the photophone was not shared by other scientists at the time. The invention worked for short distances but could not compare to the telephone's practical features which allowed for communication over great distances.

Another person who was not excited with the photophone was Mabel. She had just given birth to their second child, Marian. In a letter about the new baby, she wrote her concerns about her husband's lack of excitement toward their newest daughter:

> I fear Alec has been far too busy with his baby [the photophone] to talk or write much about mine. He thinks it is

Alexander Graham Bell places the first long-distance call from New York to Chicago. The line was opened as part of the beginning ceremonies for the 1892 Chicago Columbian Exposition.

more wonderful than the telephone, though he cannot assert it is more marvelous than this little living, human mite.[65]

At the same time that his photophone received its less-than-enthusiastic reception from his peers and his wife, Bell also received one of his greatest honors. In 1880 he was awarded the Volta Prize for inventing the telephone. The Volta Prize is an honor given by the French government to honor an outstanding invention. It was named for Italian inventor Alessandro Volta, who had invented the first battery.

Along with the praise and honor of the Volta Prize came a cash award of fifty thousand francs, which equaled about ten thousand dollars. Winning the prize was a great affirmation for Bell's work, and he used the money to organize a group of inventors to help him with new experiments. In spite of the controversy he had survived with the telephone, he was proud of how it had enhanced the world of communication. Now he was anxious to try his hand at other projects with his group of inventors, whom he named the Volta Laboratory Associates.

7 Genius Beyond the Telephone

Between 1880 and the early 1900s, Bell put the initial fame of the telephone behind him. For the rest of his life, he worked on other projects, always testing his theories with experiments. He also scheduled time for teaching and later helped form the National Geographic Society because of his desire to teach the world about the many forms of science. However, even with Bell's varied interests and his love for teaching, most people remember Alexander Graham Bell as a gifted inventor.

THE VOLTA LABORATORY ASSOCIATES

Now that Bell had his own finances devoted strictly for experiments, he made the Volta Laboratory Associates a main priority. In addition to Bell, Charles Tainter and Bell's cousin Chichester "Chester" Bell—a chemist—became the first members of the group most often referred to as the Volta Laboratory Associates.

One of the early projects that the group decided to put its collective knowledge behind was improving Thomas Edison's phonograph. The phonograph was an invention that reproduced sound using a theory with which Bell was familiar. Bell had lectured on this method of sound reproduction in the past, and he wrote a letter to Hubbard about the similarity:

> It is a most astonishing thing to me that I could possibly have let this invention slip through my fingers when I consider how my thoughts had been directed to this subject for so many years past.[66]

Based on the essential information he already had, Bell and his associates made several improvements to Edison's phonograph. The phonograph reproduced sound using a tinfoil cylinder. The cylinder had indentations in the tinfoil that plucked steel reeds when it revolved.

One problem with the tinfoil was that the indentations would wear out after being played several times. Bell and his associates came up with a wax cylinder that did not wear out when the indentations were plucked. Later, the Volta team upgraded the cylinder shape to a flat wax disc.

The Volta members made an impact in this field, and each man became quite wealthy from his contributions to the patents and marketing of the wax disc. With this success to their credit, the Volta men continued researching and making scientific discoveries. Bell stayed involved as well, giving financial, hands-on, and moral support.

INVENTIONS FROM TRAGEDIES

Shortly after the Volta team's first success, a series of dramatic events turned Bell's attention away from sound reproduction.

In July 1881 President James Garfield was shot in the back by an assassin. Since Bell had earlier used an electrical process to detect metals, he was called to the president's hospital bed in hopes that he could detect the location of the embedded bullet. The devices that had worked with telephones, however, did not work when Bell tried them on President Garfield.

Bell reworked the device and modified it to include a needlelike probe that would make clicking noises when it detected metal. Bell believed that the probe would help the doctors pinpoint the location of the bullet. To demonstrate the invention's potential to Garfield's doctors, Bell had someone hide a bullet in a slab of meat. He then activated the probe, heard clicking, and located the bullet. The demonstration worked well, but the president's doctors did not use the device. Garfield was already near death and passed away soon afterward.

Most biographers believe that the decision not to use the probe was based on Garfield's worsened condition rather than on any problems with Bell's invention. This assumption is based on the large number of doctors all across the

Bell and his associates perfected Edison's phonograph by using a wax cylinder, instead of tinfoil, to improve the durability of recordings.

world who used Bell's probe only a few years later.

While Bell had been sweltering in his Washington, D.C., laboratory working on the probe for Garfield, tragedy struck on a more personal level. On August 15, 1881, Mabel gave birth to their first son, Edward. The baby arrived prematurely and had difficulty breathing; he died within a few hours.

The Bells' second son, Robert, was born in November 1883. He, too, was premature and died soon after birth. These two deaths so close together prompted Bell to work on a device that could aid breathing. He invented an apparatus that wrapped around the chest and forced air into and out of the lungs.

Although the device never became a practical tool in Bell's lifetime, some of his theories were used to design today's more modern breathing machine, the iron lung.

OTHER MAJOR EXPERIMENTS

Bell spent much of his time in Nova Scotia at the country home he called Beinn Bhreagh. At various times throughout the year, Bell and Mabel lived in the quiet countryside, where Bell enjoyed a climate much like that of his native Scotland. The solitude allowed him to become deeply involved with his experiments, which sometimes made him wonder if he spent enough time with Mabel. After

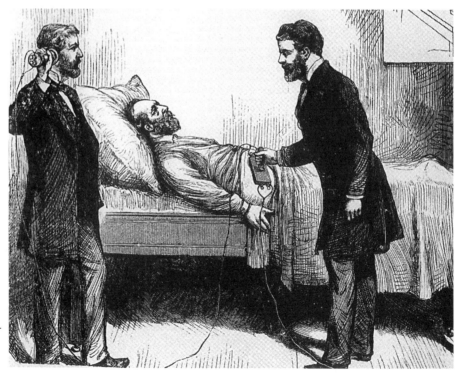

Bell invented a metal-detecting probe to help locate the assassin's bullet inside President James A. Garfield's body.

As a result of his son's death due to breathing problems, Bell invented a vacuum jacket that led to the development of the iron lung.

one visit to Beinn Bhreagh, Bell wrote his wife a note that professed his continued love, even while admitting that his attention often strayed to other matters:

> I love you more than you can ever know. I feel I have neglected you; deaf-mutes, gravitation and any other hobby has been too apt to take the first place in my thoughts. Yet, all the time my heart was yours alone. I will throw everything to one side and this summer shall be devoted to you and the children.[67]

Mabel later told a friend about his note and how he always had good intentions of spending more time with her and the family. In reality, though, Bell could never keep his attention on one thing for very long; he always had several experiments going at once.

One such experiment lasted nearly thirty years and involved sheep. Bell studied the genealogical records of his flock at Beinn Bhreagh and controlled the animals' reproduction to encourage two particular results. First, he hoped to come up with a breed that often gave birth to twins, a novelty that would double a shepherd's flock. Over time, he achieved that goal. Secondly, he hoped to develop the breed so that it also produced multiple nipples, which would be necessary for nursing twins.

When both of these goals were achieved, Bell believed that he had contributed all that he could to the project and chose to sell the flock. Mabel, however, could not stand the thought of

In February of 1909, the Silver Dart, *an engine-powered plane, rose off of the ice and flew for six minutes.*

losing all of her husband's sheep, so she instructed the family's coachman, John McDermid, to bid on a few head on her behalf. After the auction, Bell discovered the truth and was quite amused with his wife's sneaky behavior:

> Mrs. Bell was almost heartbroken over the idea of the complete disappearance of my multi-nippled sheep. . . . As this is a free country she decided, without saying anything to me upon the subject, to buy some of the sheep herself.[68]

FLYING

Since his youth, Bell had wondered whether it was possible for man to fly. His friend Samuel Langley, who was the secretary of the Smithsonian Institution, had been researching flying machines, and Bell soon became Langley's most enthusiastic student. Before long Bell had tested different types of propellers, wings, and various sources of power, including gunpowder rockets.

Bell often wrote and spoke about his experiments, sharing his thoughts about flight and the potential impact it could have on the world. In an 1893 interview with *McClure's* magazine, Bell stated,

> I have not the shadow of a doubt that the whole problem of aerial navigation will be solved within ten years. That means an entire revolution in the world's methods of transportation and of making war.[69]

Bell's statements were considered outlandish at the time, but by World War II, his words rang true as airplane missions proved to be an essential war strategy.

In 1907 Bell formed the Aerial Experiment Association (AEA) with four young men who were also interested in the possibility of flight. Within a year, they had built a glider that lifted off the ground and stayed in the air for several minutes. By 1909 the AEA's *Silver Dart,* an engine-powered plane, left the ground and flew thirty feet into the air

AN AEA EXPERIMENT EARNS A NEWSPAPER STORY

In a May 9, 1908, Herald *newspaper article included in the* Alexander Graham Bell Family Papers, *Bell comments on the Aerial Experiment Association's flight of the* White Wing.

"It was a great gratification to me to see the very promising results of the experiment made with Mr. Baldwin's Aerodrome, *White Wing*, today. It made its maiden flight, not very much in itself, but a very great thing as showing what it may do in the future. There are still difficulties to be overcome before we can go into extensive flights, but today it carried Mr. Baldwin up to a height estimated by people close at hand at ten feet. After the trial was over the distance was measured from a point where it left the ground to where it descended, and it was 93 yards. That was a pretty good maiden flight. . . .

Lieutenant Thomas Selfridge is keeping an eye on the experiments. . . . it is his duty as an officer of the army to study what is being done in the way of artificial flight both in America and abroad, and the association gets the benefit of his special knowledge in this art, by reports from time to time describing the French and other experiments."

White Wing *was just one of the many projects that Bell worked on in his later life.*

Bell and his assistants observe the progress of one of their tetrahedral kites.

for nearly an entire mile. Estimated speed was calculated at forty miles per hour.

The AEA's achievements were incredible to the average observer; however, the U. S. Army showed little interest in aviation at the time. Therefore, having accomplished what it had set out to do, the AEA disbanded.

TETRAHEDRAL KITES

Although his former AEA partners had not agreed with him, Bell believed that a kite would be the most practical and reliable source of staying in the air. His designs were complex and varied in shape, consisting of tetrahedral cells. These cells were made of lightweight wood covered in silk. With the help of his family and as-

sistants, Bell constructed and flew these tetrahedral kites for years. They remained a constant interest during the later years of his life.

HYDROFOIL WATERCRAFT

Bell's interests were not limited to flying in the air, though. He also had an idea for a boat that could go so fast that it seemed to fly across water. During his later years, Bell and his assistant Casey Baldwin, a young engineer, built hydrofoil boats. Hydrofoil boats are lightweight boats built to skim on top of the water at a fast speed.

Bell worked on the idea because of the German submarines that were sinking American ships during World War I. He hoped that his design could be modified to chase after the German submarines and destroy them, but the navy did not believe that the craft's design was functional for their purposes. One of his boats did, however, set a speed record on September 9, 1919, when the hydrofoil was clocked at nearly seventy-one miles per hour. The record stood for ten years.

ALWAYS TEACHING

In the mid-1880s, while working to help the deaf community, Bell combined his inventive mind with his teacher's sensibilities. He invented an instrument called the audiometer, which measured the hearing capabilities of children. The audiometer consisted of a telephone receiver and induction coils that sent various tones and frequencies that were heard by students. As one biographer mentions, the instrument soon became a valuable tool for measuring hearing loss in schoolchildren: "In 1885, Bell reported to the National Academy of Sciences that more than 10 per cent of 700 school children screened with the audiometer proved to have some hearing loss."[70]

A short time before his work with the audiometer, Bell founded a "dual school" called Mr. Bell's Private School. When the school opened in 1884, it was

---

BELL CONTINUES TO HELP DEAF CHILDREN

Bell's ability to help deaf children encouraged hopeful parents to seek his guidance. This letter, excerpted from the Alexander Graham Bell Family Papers, *is from Charles L. Shattuck, and it is only one of hundreds of such letters that Bell received and responded to with positive words.*

"Dear Sir,
    We have a little girl of five years, our only child, who is a congenitally deaf mute. She is strong and healthy, of sunny disposition with an active and well balanced mind. . . . How to rightly train and educate her has been a matter of deep anxiety with us. We have read with great satisfaction some writings of yours, treating upon the education of this class of children, thus gaining such valuable information. . . . Which is better, public or private instruction, and at what age ought she to enter a public school? If a public school, which public school would you recommend? I take the liberty to write you, knowing you to be authority in these matters. Trusting you will pardon this trespass upon your valuable time, I remain—
    Very truly,
    C. L. Shattuck"

the first-known school to teach both deaf and hearing children.

Each of his daughters enrolled in the new school, and soon there were so many children that more room was needed. Eventually, the school moved into a larger building. All of Bell's students were special to him, and he took an interest in each child. His sympathetic nature and successful teaching methods earned him respect and admiration, far surpassing what he had received in his early teaching career.

He took an equal interest in his own children as well, even when he could not be in the home each day with Mabel. When she once considered replacing their daughter Elsie's doll because it had broken, Bell sent a twenty-page letter to his wife:

> Should not a doll be to a child what the child is to us? To us these dolls may appear to be only painted bits of wood or sawdust bags with porcelain heads—but we should not forget that to our children they are living things—their own helpless babies.[71]

Bell's nurturing words as a parent also reflected the sensitivity that helped make him such a successful teacher.

A FAMOUS PUPIL

One of the most famous deaf students whom Bell helped was Helen Keller. Keller would later become one of the most well known deaf persons in the world. She and Bell remained close friends

Alexander Graham Bell worked with Helen Keller, who would always remember him fondly.

throughout his life, and she credited Bell with her success as a writer, speaker, and advocate of the deaf. Many biographers have recorded Keller's first visit to Bell, which emphasized his tender nature and willingness to help his students.

In 1887 Helen Keller's parents brought her from Alabama to Bell's Washington, D.C., school. Six-year-old Helen was not only deaf but also blind. Helen's weary mother and father escorted her into Bell's office, watching as

BELL'S COMMENTS ABOUT HELEN KELLER'S PROGRESS

In a letter dated January 21, 1892, Bell praised Anne Sullivan for her work with Helen Keller and commented on Sullivan's methods of teaching young Helen. This letter is part of the Alexander Graham Bell Family Papers.

"Dear Miss Sullivan:—Allow me to thank you for the privilege of reading your account of how you taught Helen Keller. . . . I am particularly struck by your statement that you gave Helen books printed in raised letters 'long before she could read them,' and that 'she would amuse herself for hours each day in carefully passing her fingers over the words, searching for such words as she knew,' etc.

I consider that statement as of very great significance and importance when I try to account for her wonderful familiarity with idiomatic English. She is such an exceptional child that we are apt to attribute everything to her marvellous mind, and forget that language comes from without, and not from within. . . .

The great problem in the education of the deaf is the teaching of idiomatic language.

I am sure that instructors of the deaf will support me in urging you to tell us all you can as to the part played by books in the instruction of Helen Keller."

Helen Keller, Annie Sullivan, and Alexander Graham Bell.

she moved in a frustrated manner around the room. As Helen "saw" Bell's office with her hands, her mother explained how difficult the child was to manage.

Helen was a whirlwind of motion, touching and exploring everything with her fingers. The young girl's need to feel everything that she could not see or hear embarrassed her parents. But Bell immediately understood young Helen's sense of wonderment. He embraced the girl and she relaxed, then snuggled Bell's neck. Her parents were amazed. Their daughter had never shown such open trust and peace with anyone.

After the hug, Bell allowed Helen to continue roaming around his office. As she did, he studied her actions. Bell told her parents that he believed their daughter was quite intelligent and suggested that they enroll her at the Perkins Institute for the Blind in Boston. Bell also told the Kellers that he wanted to be updated on Helen's progress. In Boston, Helen met Anne Sullivan, who helped her learn how to experience and enjoy life even with her disabilities.

For many years after that initial meeting, Keller often visited Bell. Throughout her life, she credited him with being the first to see and comprehend the sensitive and inquisitive child she was. She always believed that Bell was the one person who helped free her from being trapped behind a dark curtain of blindness and silence. She later wrote to Bell, sharing her feelings about the impact he had on her life:

Even before my teacher came, you held out a hand to me in the dark. I have not forgotten how you followed step by step my teacher's efforts to free my mind, my life, my heart from the tyranny of circumstance. . . . When others who had little faith in the power of spirit to conquer blindness doubted and faltered, it was you who heartened us for the struggle.[72]

Keller's words echo sentiments expressed by many of the deaf students whom Bell encouraged. Even with such high praise from Helen Keller, Bell soon discovered that one particular individual was not pleased with his methods of instruction.

ANOTHER CLOUD OF CONTROVERSY

A man named Edward M. Gallaudet, who was also highly respected in the field of deaf education, preferred to teach his pupils sign language. Bell, however, believed that deaf people should be taught to read lips and to speak. He felt that a system of communication that separated the deaf from the hearing was not in a deaf person's best interest.

Bell's system of education invited the deaf to be part of society rather than isolating them in separate schools. Gallaudet disagreed and attacked Bell by challenging his credentials in heated public debates.

Further personal attacks on Bell's honesty and integrity arose, once again concerning the original telephone patents. The U. S. government filed a lawsuit against Bell based on false information provided by the Pan-Electric Company accusing the inventor of bribing patent offical Zenas Frank Wilber to file his claim to the talking telegraph before any others. Bell was so infuriated by the lawsuit that his statement to the court was filled with passion as he blatantly denied the charges. Bell's statement was later reprinted in the *Washington Post,* with Bell's strong drama ringing clear: "I never presented, paid, gave, or handed to Zenas Frank Wilber . . . any money, or any valuable consideration or thing whatever for any purpose."[73]

Some biographers believe that these controversies caused Bell to retreat to Beinn Bhreagh and spend less time teaching deaf students. But even as Bell spent more time in Nova Scotia, he continued to write letters so that he could stay in touch with his friends in the United States. When his early pupil George Sanders's father, Thomas, passed away, Bell sent his condolences and reflected on his fondness for the Sanders family and its influence on his first years in Boston:

> My dear George:
> I have not the heart to reply to your note of August 5 after the shock of your telegram about your father's death. I begin to feel very old. There is hardly anyone left of all the friends with whom I was so intimate in 1872 when you little fellow, five years of

age, came into my life. You are my last remaining link connecting me with those happy Salem days when your dear Grandmother was alive. I often look back and think of those times . . . and now your father's death comes as a great shock. He was not only a dear personal friend but the first in the world to take practical interest in the telephone and helped me out. He and Mr. Hubbard together assumed all my financial liabilities for experimental work on the telephone and organized the first telephone companies.[74]

A WIDER MEANS OF COMMUNICATION

Also while in Beinn Bhreagh, as he was throughout his entire life, Bell was an avid reader of a great many scientific magazines and journals. At one point he even helped the financially troubled *Science* magazine after Thomas Edison stopped funding the publication. In 1882 Bell and his father-in-law rescued the magazine by pumping their own funds into the publication. It was ultimately turned over to the American Association for the Advancement of Science and became the association's official journal.

THE NATIONAL GEOGRAPHIC SOCIETY

Another science journal that Bell contributed to was an extension of a group that Hubbard encouraged Bell to form. The

Alexander Graham Bell (center) at the ceremonies opening the first transcontinental telephone line.

popular *National Geographic* magazine on newsstands today grew from a small group of men who wanted to share all types of sciences and explorations with the world.

Hubbard thought a group of great thinkers and explorers was needed in Washington, D.C., and he even suggested a name: the National Geographic Society. Arctic adventurer A. W. Greely attended the first meeting and joined the new organization. Greely, along with thirty-three other men, elected Hubbard as the president. Hubbard accepted the presidency and announced the society's main objective: to fund, explore, and share information.

By my election, you notify the public that the membership of our society will not be confined to professional geographers, but will include that large number who, like myself, desire to promote special researches by others and to diffuse the knowledge so gained, among men, so that we may know more of the world upon which we live.[75]

Hubbard remained president for ten years, until his death in December 1897. After much pressure from his mother-in-law, Bell agreed to take over the presidency of the society. However, given

Bell's passion for wondering about his next experiments, he soon lost interest in the inner workings of both the society and the magazine schedule.

In March 1899 Bell convinced Gilbert Grosvenor to take on the day-to-day operations as his assistant. Bell continued to contribute articles to the magazine, but he remained in the shadows of public life until 1915, when the telephone reached a new milestone.

COAST-TO-COAST TELEPHONE SERVICE

On January 25, 1915, Bell, who was stationed in New York, placed a telephone call to Thomas Watson, who was awaiting the call in San Francisco, California.

Bell's words were transmitted across three thousand miles of telephone wire before they completed the circuit. Watson heard his telephone ring and picked up the receiver. Once more he listened to his old partner announce, "Hoy, Hoy, Mr. Watson are you there? Do you hear me?"[76]

With the transcontinental telephone transmission a success and his dream achieved, Bell once again set his sights on the future. His next project was not as important to the world as it was to Belle's grandson, Melville.

The aging inventor worked to develop a few simple experiments for his grandson. He decided to focus on this project because the boy showed little interest in

To honor the great inventor, as Bell was buried in Nova Scotia, telephone service was halted temporarily on the 13 million telephones in the United States and Canada.

Sadness, but No Mourning for Bell

In a letter to her sister, included in Edwin S. Grosvenor's biography of Bell, Marian Bell shares the events of their father's death. She also gives insight into the manner in which her mother handled the loss of her husband, the famous inventor.

"He pressed mother's hand almost to the end—and very shortly before he died when Mother was calling him, he opened his eyes and we all knew he had come back and knew her. . . .

She goes on just as usual—makes all the motions—laughs and talks but you never forget for a moment that the heart of everything had gone out of life for her forever. . . .

She isn't wearing mourning. She says she could never take it off if she did. . . . Mother stepped forward and stood alone with her arm resting on the coffin—bare-headed and in white with a soft white scarf around her neck. . . .

The children played about and ran up and down stairs—there was no feeling at all that death was terrible."

Alexander Graham Bell and his grandchildren.

science. Bell wanted young Melville to discover the same love of science that had prompted him to pursue his dream of reproducing human speech. Without that childhood sense of wonder, Bell might not have gone on to invent the telephone.

Today the telephone continues to play a key role in everyday life. It allows people to speak to one another across great distances. It gives immediate access to the Internet and to e-mail messages. It even sends facsimile transmissions across the oceans in seconds. Because of Alexander Graham Bell's telephone, worldwide communication is a reality.

On August 22, 1922, the man who devoted his life to invention died of anemia, a lack of blood circulation brought on by diabetes. He was buried at the top of his favorite hill on Beinn Bhreagh in Nova Scotia. The stone marking his grave lists Bell's date of birth and death, along with one simple message: Inventor.

Notes

Introduction: Communication and Invention

1. May Hill Arbuthnot and Dorothy M. Broderick, eds., *Time for Biography.* Glenview, IL: Scott, Foresman, 1969, p. 115.
2. Quoted in Ernest V. Heyn, *Fire of Genius.* Garden City, NY: Anchor, 1976, p. 66.
3. Quoted in Heyn, *Fire of Genius,* p. 49.

Chapter 1: A Family of Communicators

4. Edwin S. Grosvenor, *Alexander Graham Bell: The Life and Times of the Man Who Invented the Telephone.* New York: Harry N. Abrams, 1997, p. 17.
5. Quoted in Heyn, *Fire of Genius,* p. 50.
6. Grosvenor, *Alexander Graham Bell,* p. 15.
7. Quoted in Grosvenor, *Alexander Graham Bell,* p. 17.
8. Quoted in Grosvenor, *Alexander Graham Bell,* p. 16.
9. Quoted in Grosvenor, *Alexander Graham Bell,* p. 17.
10. Quoted in Thomas B. Costain, *The Chord of Steel.* Garden City, NY: Doubleday, 1960, p. 30.
11. Quoted in Costain, *The Chord of Steel,* p. 32.
12. Quoted in Grosvenor, *Alexander Graham Bell,* p. 17.
13. Quoted in Grosvenor, *Alexander Graham Bell,* p. 22.
14. Quoted in Grosvenor, *Alexander Graham Bell,* p. 22.
15. Quoted in Grosvenor, *Alexander Graham Bell,* p. 23.
16. Quoted in Grosvenor, *Alexander Graham Bell,* p. 23.

Chapter 2: A Love for Teaching

17. Quoted in O. J. Stevenson, *The Talking Wire.* New York: Julian Messner, 1947, p. 55.
18. Quoted in Grosvenor, *Alexander Graham Bell,* p. 29.
19. Quoted in Grosvenor, *Alexander Graham Bell,* p. 30.
20. Quoted in Grosvenor, *Alexander Graham Bell,* p. 30.
21. Quoted in Grosvenor, *Alexander Graham Bell,* p. 30.
22. Quoted in Stevenson, *The Talking Wire,* p. 65.
23. Quoted in Grosvenor, *Alexander Graham Bell,* p. 32.
24. Quoted in Grosvenor, *Alexander Graham Bell,* p. 33.
25. Quoted in Grosvenor, *Alexander Graham Bell,* p. 33.

Chapter 3: Respected Teacher and Researcher

26. Stevenson, *The Talking Wire,* p. 70.
27. Quoted in Helen Waite, *Make a Joyful Sound.* Philadelphia: Macrae Smith, 1961, p. 70.
28. Quoted in Waite, *Make a Joyful Sound,* p. 71.
29. Quoted in Grosvenor, *Alexander Graham Bell,* p. 36.
30. Quoted in Waite, *Make a Joyful Sound,* p. 72.
31. Quoted in Waite, *Make a Joyful Sound,*

p. 75.

32. Alexander G. Bell, October 1, 1872, *Alexander Graham Bell Family Papers*, American Memory Collection, Library of Congress,
p. 2. http://memory.loc.gov/ammem/bell.html/bellsp.html.

33. Quoted in Grosvenor, *Alexander Graham Bell*, pp. 42–43.

34. Heyn, *Fire of Genius*, pp. 55–56.

35. Grosvenor, *Alexander Graham Bell*, p. 39.

Chapter 4: Inventing the Telephone

36. Quoted in Heyn, *Fire of Genius*, p. 56.

37. Quoted in Costain, *The Chord of Steel*, p. 116.

38. Quoted in Heyn, *Fire of Genius*, p. 57.

39. Quoted in Costain, *The Chord of Steel*, p. 122.

40. Quoted in Grosvenor, *Alexander Graham Bell*, p. 67.

41. Quoted in Grosvenor, *Alexander Graham Bell*, p. 67.

42. Quoted in Costain, *The Chord of Steel*, p. 124.

43. Quoted in Costain, *The Chord of Steel*, p. 125.

44. Quoted in Grosvenor, *Alexander Graham Bell*, p. 69.

45. Quoted in Waite, *Make a Joyful Sound*, p. 119.

Chapter 5: Introducing the Telephone to the World

46. Quoted in Waite, *Make a Joyful Sound*, p. 132.

47. Quoted in Grosvenor, *Alexander Graham Bell*, p. 71.

48. Quoted in Heyn, *Fire of Genius*, p. 61.

49. Quoted in Grosvenor, *Alexander Graham Bell*, p. 72.

50. Quoted in Heyn, *Fire of Genius*, p. 66.

51. Quoted in Grosvenor, *Alexander Graham Bell*, p. 73.

52. Quoted in Costain, *The Chord of Steel*, p. 193.

53. Grosvenor, *Alexander Graham Bell*, p. 75.

54. Heyn, *Fire of Genius*, p. 66.

55. Quoted in Grosvenor, *Alexander Graham Bell*, p. 79.

56. Quoted in Grosvenor, *Alexander Graham Bell*, p. 88.

Chapter 6: Mass Communication and Controversy

57. Quoted in Waite, *Make a Joyful Sound*, p. 163.

58. Quoted in Grosvenor, *Alexander Graham Bell*, p. 121.

59. Grosvenor, *Alexander Graham Bell*, p. 92.

60. Quoted in Waite, *Make a Joyful Sound*, p. 171.

61. Quoted in Waite, *Make a Joyful Sound*, p. 171.

62. Quoted in Grosvenor, *Alexander Graham Bell*, p. 93.

63. Quoted in Grosvenor, *Alexander Graham Bell*, p. 93.

64. Quoted in Heyn, *Fire of Genius*, p. 74.

65. Quoted in Grosvenor, *Alexander Graham Bell*, p. 104.

Chapter 7: Genius Beyond the Telephone

66. Quoted in Grosvenor, *Alexander Graham Bell*, p. 110.

67. Quoted in Grosvenor, *Alexander Graham Bell*, p. 114.

68. Quoted in Grosvenor, *Alexander Graham Bell*, p. 265

69. Quoted in Grosvenor, *Alexander Graham Bell*, p. 141.

70. Heyn, *Fire of Genius*, p. 79.

71. Quoted in Grosvenor, *Alexander Graham Bell*, p. 112.

72. Quoted in Grosvenor, *Alexander Graham Bell*, p. 158.

73. Quoted in Grosvenor, *Alexander Graham Bell*, p. 113.

74. Alexander G. Bell, August 14, 1911, *Alexander Graham Bell Family Papers*.

75. Quoted in Grosvenor, *Alexander Graham Bell*, p. 185.

76. Quoted in Grosvenor, *Alexander Graham Bell*, p. 243.

For Further Reading

Margaret Davidson, *The Story of Alexander Graham Bell: Inventor of the Telephone*. Milwaukee: Gareth Stevens, 1997. Presented in a story format, this book outlines Bell's entire life.

Dorothy H. Eber, *Genius at Work*. New York: Viking, 1982. A beautiful pictorial tribute to Bell's last years spent in Nova Scotia developing many of his varied experiments.

Joseph and Frances Gies, *The Ingenius Yankees*. New York: Thomas Crowell, 1976. A collective biography that details the lives and inventions of America's greatest inventors.

Naomi Pasachoff, *Alexander Graham Bell Making Connections*. New York: Oxford University Press, 1996. A well-rounded, easy-to-read biography presented in a chronological format for young adults.

Patricia R. Quiri, *Alexander Graham Bell*. New York: Franklin Watts, 1991. A juvenile edition giving a basic overview of Bell's life and major inventions.

Katherine B. Shippen, *Mr. Bell Meets the Telephone*. New York: Random House, 1952. Using a story format, this book revolves around Bell's work on the telephone.

Ralph Stein, *The Great Inventions*. Chicago: Ridge, 1976. A beautiful coffee table book that boasts many of the world's greatest inventions, how they came about, and brief biographies of their inventors.

Works Consulted

Books

May Hill Arbuthnot and Dorothy M. Broderick, eds., *Time for Biography.* Glenview, IL: Scott, Foresman, 1969. A collective biography of many famous people, centering on why those people are famous.

Thomas B. Costain, *The Chord of Steel.* Garden City, NY: Doubleday, 1960. A partial biography highlighting Bell's earlier career, with strong emphasis on Bell's connection to his father's Canadian home.

Edwin S. Grosvenor, *Alexander Graham Bell: The Life and Times of the Man Who Invented the Telephone.* New York: Harry N. Abrams, 1997. A thorough biography full of gorgeous photos that gives an in-depth look at Bell's professional and personal life.

Ernest V. Heyn, *Fire of Genius.* Garden City, NY: Anchor, 1976. A collective biography of inventors, offering substantial life overviews of the inventors as well as plentiful photographs of the machines they invented.

Jerome S. Meyer, *World Book of Great Inventors.* Cleveland: World, 1956. A collective biography that lists more about the actual inventions than the inventors.

O. J. Stevenson, *The Talking Wire.* New York: Julian Messner, 1947. Concentrates on A. G. Bell's life in Brantford when he returned home from teaching in Boston and perfected his telephone invention.

Helen Waite, *Make a Joyful Sound.* Philadelphia: Macrae Smith, 1961. An extremely well researched biography about Mabel and Alexander Bell writen in cooperation with their children. It includes many entries from Mabel's diaries and the correspondence between Mabel and Bell throughout their courtship and marriage.

Holland Thompson and Arthur Mee, ed., *The Book of Knowledge: The Children's Encyclopedia.* New York: Grolier, 1940. One volume in a set of encyclopedias that are easy to read and basic in format and topic.

Internet Source

Alexander Graham Bell Family Papers, American Memory Collection, Library of Congress..http://memory.loc.gov/ammem/bellhtml/bellsp.html. A full collection of all of Bell's diary entries, experiment notebooks, and letters.

Index

Picture Credits

Cover Photo: Corbis
AT&T Archives, 87, 104
Corbis, 37
Corbis/Bettmann, 24
Library of Congress, 12, 14, 15, 17, 19, 22, 23 ,25, 26, 28, 29, 31, 32, 33, 34, 36, 39, 42, 44, 46, 48, 51, 52, 53, 54, 55, 56, 57, 58, 62, 63, 64, 65, 68, 70, 74, 78, 82, 83, 84, 89, 90, 93, 94, 95, 96, 97, 98, 101, 105, 106
PhotoDisc, 11, 13
Prints Old and Rare, 80
Western Electric, 44

About the Author

Robyn M. Weaver is a writer, editor, and Continuing Education instructor at Texas Christian University. She travels across the country, leading seminars about the mechanics of writing and also giving workshops on how to use writing exercises to help heal emotional wounds.